ESSENTIALS OF
FORENSIC SCIENCE

Trace Evidence

Max M. Houck

SET EDITOR
Suzanne Bell, Ph.D.

An imprint of Infobase Publishing

Facts On File, Inc.
An imprint of Infobase Publishing
132 West 31st Street
New York NY 10001

Library of Congress Cataloging-in-Publication Data
Houck, Max M.
   Trace evidence / Max M. Houck.
     p. cm.—(Essentials of forensic science)
   Includes bibliographical references and index.
   ISBN-13: 978-0-8160-5511-1
   ISBN-10: 0-8160-5511-4
   1. Trace analysis. 2. Forensic sciences. 3. Evidence, Criminal. I. Title.
   HV8073.H779 2008
   363.25'62—dc22   2008012786

Facts On File books are available at special discounts when purchased in bulk quantities for businesses, associations, institutions, or sales promotions. Please call our Special Sales Department in New York at (212) 967-8800 or (800) 322-8755.

You can find Facts On File on the World Wide Web at http://www.factsonfile.com

Text design by Erik Lindstrom
Illustrations by Lucidity Information Design
Photo research by Suzanne M. Tibor
Composition by Mark Lerner
Cover printed by Bang Printing, Brainerd, MN
Book printed and bound by Bang Printing, Brainerd, MN
Date printed: April, 2010
Printed in the United States of America

10 9 8 7 6 5 4 3 2

This book is printed on acid-free paper.

This book is dedicated to the memories of Michael Grieve, Barry Gaudette, and Jim Crocker, from whom I learned a great deal, whether they knew they were teaching me or not.

CONTENTS

PREFACE

Forensic science has become in the early 21st century what the space race was in the 1960s—an accessible and inspiring window into the world of science. The surge in popularity that began in the latter part of the 20th century echoes a boom that began in the later part of the 19th century and was labeled the "Sherlock Holmes effect." Today it is called the "C.S.I. effect," but the consequences are the same as they were a century ago. The public has developed a seemingly insatiable appetite for anything forensic, be it fiction, reality, or somewhere between.

Essentials of Forensic Science is a set that is written in response to this thirst for knowledge and information. Written by eminent forensic scientists, the books cover the critical core of forensic science from its earliest inception to the modern laboratory and courtroom.

Forensic science is broadly defined as the application of science to legal matters, be they criminal cases or civil lawsuits. The history of the law dates back to the earliest civilizations, such as the Sumerians and the Egyptians, starting around 5000 B.C.E. The roots of science are older than civilization. Early humans understood how to make tools, how to cook food, how to distinguish between edible and inedible plants, and how to make rudimentary paints. This knowledge was technical and not based on any underlying unifying principles. The core of these behaviors is the drive to learn, which as a survival strategy was invaluable. Humans learned to cope with different environments and conditions, allowing adaptation when other organisms could not. Ironically, the information encoded in human DNA gives us the ability to analyze, classify, and type it.

Science as a formalized system of thinking can be traced to the ancient Greeks, who were the first to impose systematic patterns of thought and analysis to observations. This occurred around 500 B.C.E. The Greeks organized ideas about the natural world and were able to conceive of advanced concepts. They postulated the atom (from the

Greek word *atomos*) as the fundamental unit of all matter. The Greeks were also among the first to study anatomy, medicine, and physiology in a systematic way and to leave extensive written records of their work. They also formalized the concept of the autopsy.

From ancient roots to modern practice the history of forensic science winds through the Middle Ages, alchemy, and the fear of poisoning. In 1840 pivotal scientific testimony was given by Mathieu-Joseph-Bonaventure (Mateu Josep Bonaventura) Orfila (1787–1853) in a trial in Paris related to a suspected case of arsenic poisoning. His scientific technique and testimony marks the beginning of modern forensic science. Today the field is divided into specialties such as biology (DNA analysis), chemistry, firearms and tool marks, questioned documents, toxicology, and pathology. This division is less than a half-century old. In Orfila's time the first to practice forensic science were doctors, chemists, lawyers, investigators, biologists, and microscopists with other skills and interests that happened to be of use to the legal system. Their testimony was and remains opinion testimony, something the legal system was slow to embrace. Early courts trusted swearing by oath—better still if oaths of others supported it. Eyewitnesses were also valued, even if their motives were less than honorable. Only in the last century has the scientific expert been integrated into the legal arena with a meaningful role. Essentials of Forensic Science is a distillation of the short history and current status of modern forensic science.

The set is divided into seven volumes:

☑ *Science versus Crime* by Max Houck, director of research — forensic science, West Virginia University; Fellow, American Academy of Forensic Sciences; formerly of the FBI (trace evidence analyst/anthropologist), working at the Pentagon and Waco. This book covers the important cases and procedures that govern scientific evidence, the roles of testimony and admissibility hearings, and how the law and scientific evidence intersect in a courtroom.

☑ *Blood, Bugs, and Plants* by Dr. R. E. Gaensslen, professor, forensic science; head of program and director of graduate studies; Distinguished Fellow, American Academy of Forensic

Sciences; former editor of the *Journal of Forensic Sciences*. This book delves into the many facets of forensic biology. Topics include a historical review of forensic serology (ABO blood groups), DNA typing, forensic entomology, forensic ecology, and forensic botany.

☑ *Drugs, Poisons, and Chemistry* by Dr. Suzanne Bell, Bennett Department of Chemistry, West Virginia University; Fellow of the American Board of Criminalistics; and Fellow of the American Academy of Forensics. This book covers topics in forensic chemistry, including an overview of drugs and poisons, both as physical evidence and obtained as substances in the human body. Also included is a history of poisoning and toxicology.

☑ *Trace Evidence* by Max Houck. This book examines the common types of microscopic techniques used in forensic science, including scanning electron microscopy and analysis of microscopic evidence, such as dust, building materials, and other types of trace evidence.

☑ *Firearms and Fingerprints* by Edward Hueske, University of North Texas; supervising criminalist, Department of Public Safety of Arizona, 1983–96 (retired); Fellow, American Academy of Forensic Sciences; emeritus member of American Society of Crime Laboratory Directors (ASCLD). This book focuses on how firearms work, how impressions are created on bullets and casings, microscopic examination and comparison, and gunshot residue. The examination of other impression evidence, such as tire and shoe prints and fingerprints, is also included.

☑ *Crashes and Collapses* by Dr. Tom Bohan, J. D.; Diplomate, International Institute of Forensic Engineering Sciences; Founders Award recipient of the Engineering Sciences Section, American Academy of Forensic Sciences. This book covers forensic engineering and the investigation of accidents such as building and bridge collapses; accident reconstruction, and transportation disasters.

☑ *Fakes and Forgeries* by Dr. Suzanne Bell. This book provides an overview of questioned documents, identification of handwriting, counterfeiting, famous forgeries of art, and historical hoaxes.

Each volume begins with an overview of the subject, followed by a discussion of the history of the field and mention of the pioneers. Since the early forensic scientists were often active in several areas, the same names will appear in more than one volume. A section on the scientific principles and tools summarizes how forensic scientists working in that field acquire and apply their knowledge. With that foundation in place the forensic application of those principles is described to include important cases and the projected future in that area.

Finally, it is important to note that the volumes and the set as a whole are not meant to serve as a comprehensive textbook on the subject. Rather, the set is meant as a "pocket reference" best used for obtaining an overview of a particular subject while providing a list of resources for those needing or wanting more. The content is directed toward nonscientists, students, and members of the public who have been caught up in the current popularity of forensic science and want to move past fiction into forensic reality.

ACKNOWLEDGMENTS

I want to thank my wife, Lucy, for understanding my bouts of alternating joy and grief during this project. All of my students in my courses at West Virginia University deserve thanks for helping me to understand, explain, reduce, refine, and reabsorb the fundamentals of what forensic science is. Students are always the best teachers; you can quote me on that. I must thank the tireless efforts of Frank Darmstadt, executive editor, to work with me to get the manuscript into shape, and Suzie Tibor, who brought a professional touch to conducting photo research. Finally, I want to thank my agent, Jodie Rhodes, for keeping me in line; I'm sorry I make you work so hard, Jodie.

INTRODUCTION

Hairs from a dog in Australia help to convict a young man for killing his mother and her husband. Carpet fibers from an automobile lead police to a serial child rapist. Two men are in a car when it crashes—one dies and the survivor says the dead man was driving, but clothing fibers and impressions from a pair of jeans determine if he is telling the truth. Tiny fiber fragments seal the fate of a man who kidnapped, molested, and killed a young girl. A single hair tips the scales of a killer's conscience and convinces him to confess.

Evidence that can barely be seen with the naked eye routinely plays a part in the search for and conviction of some of the most dangerous criminals known to society. How do forensic scientists know what to look for? How do they identify these miniscule bits of debris that give the courts and jury the information they need?

Trace Evidence is about the science of trace evidence and the forensic analysis of hairs and fibers. In plain terms, trace evidence is the bits of stuff that break off from a source and transfer to another location, sticking there until removed. Forensic analysts can trace these bits to their source (most of the time) and demonstrate the association between the source and the location where they were found. Two of the most commonly found types of trace evidence, and those that are the focus of this book, are hairs and fibers.

Hairs are a complicated biological structure and can make good evidence, whether they come from animals or humans. Using a microscope, a forensic scientist can tell a lot about a hair, including what part of the body it came from and whether it was cut with scissors or a razor. New types of DNA methods can analyze hairs for their genetic content, unlike older methods. Textile fibers have been with humans ever since our species left the tropics and needed clothing for warmth and protection. Fibers come from diverse natural sources, such as plants and animals, as well as "unnatural" sources: human industry. Many modern fibers are manufactured and some are entirely synthetic (made from chemical processes).

It is the forensic analyst's role to study these trace materials and interpret them for use in legal proceedings. Hairs and fibers are first analyzed with a microscope and then by other means: DNA for hairs, chemistry instrumentation for fibers. It is important to understand the methods used to scrutinize hairs and fibers because what a forensic scientist can or cannot say in court comes directly from those methods. A faulty analysis or a wrong interpretation can send the wrong person to jail or release a deadly criminal back into society. On television, forensic science is portrayed as a matter of sexy outfits, cool sunglasses, and quick science. In practice, forensic science can involve long hours of painstaking examination, gory details, and unpleasant circumstances. But it is a powerful method of assisting the courts in handing out justice, and is not to be taken lightly.

Trace Evidence covers two types of trace evidence: hairs and fibers. It may seem strange to focus on only two types of evidence but, as you will see, the complexity of just these two materials is enough to fill a book! To cover all the types of trace evidence would take many more books. Most materials, most things, are much more complicated than people imagine—the objects in our daily lives are taken for granted. Forensic scientists must learn a lot about many things to do their job well. Understanding the importance of two minute types of evidence is key to appreciating how very small things can make a big difference in criminal investigations. Details are terribly important. More important is seeing those details in the context of the case and from the perspective of someone who understands what he or she is looking at. If a scientist does not understand the difference between nylon 6 and nylon 6,6, they will not work a case properly.

In the last few years I have realized just how much being an anthropologist has affected my views on evidence, forensic science, and the fundamentals of this profession. Looking for small bones made me appreciate trace evidence. Understanding human variation through the analysis of skeletal remains prepared me to see the value of hair examinations. Thinking of human-made objects as artifacts, when I was an archaeologist, gave me a social perspective on fibers, textiles, and their distribution across the world markets. It is remarkable that you do not always realize where your influences come from until later in your career. My time in a medical examiner's office and morgue broadened my view of what was possible in a criminal investigation—without too many gory details, it was a tremendous but horrifying experience. It left me with a very placid sense of what is possible for one person to do to another during a crime: I am hard to shock or surprise at this point. Working at the FBI Laboratory was thrilling, but also a luxury in that I was allowed to specialize in hairs, fibers, fabric, and rope. That is all I did for seven years, with a little anthropology thrown in. Specialization gave me the insights about the complexity of modern materials, and I quickly realized I could spend the rest of my life studying any single one of those things, let alone all four.

I hope that my broader, multidisciplinary view provides the reader with a better sense of what forensic science is and what it is not. Forensic science is an excellent way to learn about the world around us, those objects in it, and how to better study them through chemistry, biology, microscopy, and other methods.

What Is Evidence?

Evidence can be defined as information given in a legal investigation that makes a fact or proposition more or less likely. Whether in the form of personal testimony, the language of documents, or the production of material objects, evidence is critical to a trial. It provides the foundation for the arguments the attorneys plan to offer. It is viewed as the impartial, objective, and sometimes stubborn information that leads a judge or jury to their conclusions.

Whoever determines guilt or innocence is called the trier-of-fact, whether it is a judge or jury. In a trial, the trier-of-fact hears the statements of the case to decide the issues. This person or body must also decide if the statements made by witnesses are true or not, mainly by evaluating the information or evidence presented at trial. Suppose, for example, that the trier-of-fact hears the following information at trial: Someone was seen leaving the scene of a homicide with a knife, and scientific examination later showed that blood removed from the knife came from the victim. This could be considered evidence that this person committed the homicide. Having the association of the blood with the knife makes the proposition that the accused is the murderer more probable than it would be if the evidence did not exist. Evidence can be a complicated thing, and much goes into getting evidence ready before it can go into court.

THE DIFFERENT KINDS OF EVIDENCE

Most evidence is real; that is, it is generated as a part of the crime and recovered at the scene or at a place where the suspect or victim had been before or after the crime. Hairs, fingerprints, paint, blood, and shoeprints are all real evidence. Sometimes, however, items of evidence may be created to augment or explain real evidence. For example, diagrams of hair characteristics, a computer simulation of a crime scene, or a demonstration of bloodstain pattern mechanics may be prepared to help the trier-of-fact understand complex testimony. Such demonstrative evidence is not generated directly from the incident, but is created later. Because it helps explain the significance of real evidence, however, it does help make a proposition more or less probable. It is, therefore, evidence.

Circumstantial evidence is evidence based on inference and not on personal knowledge or observation. Most real evidence (blood, hairs, bullets, fibers, fingerprints) is circumstantial. People may think that circumstantial evidence is weak—think of television dramas where the attorney declares, "We only have a circumstantial case." But except when someone directly witnesses a crime, all cases are circumstantial cases. Given enough of the right kind of evidence, a circumstantial case could be a strong one. In particular, conclusive evidence strengthens a case. Conclusive evidence is evidence so strong as to overshadow any other evidence to the contrary. Another type of helpful evidence is called corroborating evidence. This is evidence that differs from but strengthens or confirms other evidence. For example, finding fingerprints and fibers and a bag in a suspect's possession with money whose serial numbers match those of money stolen from a bank are pieces of evidence that corroborate one another. If the evidence, on the other hand, pointed to someone other than the suspect and therefore indicated his or her innocence, that would be exculpatory evidence.

There are also types of evidence that do not strengthen a case. One such is conflicting evidence, which is irreconcilable evidence that comes from different sources. Conflicting evidence confuses the issues in the case and hampers the trier-of-fact's efforts to reach a clear decision. Another kind of unhelpful evidence is called tainted evidence, which is evidence that is discovered as a result of an illegal search (for example, where there is no proper search warrant, as outlined by the Fourth Amendment of the Constitution). Tainted evidence is inadmissible in court. Likewise, any further evidence obtained as a result of tainted evidence is also inadmissible because of the primary taint. This second kind of tainted evidence is called derivative evidence. Finally, hearsay testimony adds nothing to the strength of a case. Hearsay is testimony given by a witness who tells not what he or she knows personally, but what others have said. (This would be like one student, "Amy," telling the teacher that her friend, "Becky," could not hand in her homework because Becky told Amy her dog ate it.) Because it is dependent on the credibility of someone other than the witness, and that person is not testifying, hearsay evidence is routinely not allowed in court.

Not all evidence is on equal grounds—some items of evidence have more importance than others. The context of the crime and the type, amount, and quality of the evidence will dictate what can be determined and interpreted. Most of the items in one's daily life are mass-produced, including biological materials (one has thousands of hairs on the body, for example). This limits what can be said about the relationships between people, places, and things surrounding a crime.

FORENSIC SCIENCE IS A HISTORICAL SCIENCE

Forensic science is a science in which the events in question have already occurred and are in the past. Forensic scientists do not view the crime as it occurs (unless they are witnesses); rather, they assist the investigation by analyzing the physical remains of the criminal activity. Many sciences, such as geology, astronomy, archaeology, paleontology, and evolutionary biology, work in the same way—no evidence is seen as it is created. Rather, these scientists study only the remains of those events that are left behind. Scientists who study ancient climates (paleoclimatologists) call these remains proxy data because they represent the original data. (When someone is given the authority to represent someone else, this representative is called a proxy.)

THREE HISTORICAL SCIENCES COMPARED

	Forensic Science	Archaeology	Geology
Time frame	hours, days, months	hundreds to thousands of years	millions of years
Activity Level	personal; individual	social; populations	global
Proxy data	mass-produced	handmade	natural

Note: Forensic science is a historical science because it reconstructs past events from the physical remnants ("proxy data") of those events. In this way, forensic science is similar to other historical sciences such as geology, astronomy, paleontology, and archaeology.

Many sciences routinely analyze proxy data, although they may not refer to it as that per se. Archaeologists, for example, analyze cultural artifacts of past civilizations to interpret their activities and practices. Likewise, forensic scientists analyze evidence of past criminal events to interpret the actions of the perpetrator(s) and victim(s). The table above compares differences between some historical sciences.

Just as archaeologists must sift through layers of soil and debris to find the few items of interest at an archaeological site, so forensic scientists must sort through all of the items at a crime scene (think of all the things in the average bedroom, for example) to find the few items of evidence that will help reconstruct the crime. The nature and circumstances of the crime will guide the crime scene investigators and the forensic scientists to choose the most relevant evidence and examinations.

TRANSFER AND PERSISTENCE: THE BASIS OF ALL EVIDENCE

When two objects come into contact, some sort of information is exchanged. This basic principle is the core guiding theory of forensic science. Developed in the early 20th century by Edmund Locard, a French forensic scientist, it posits that this exchange of information occurs even if the results are not identifiable or are too small to be found. The results of such a transfer—the remnants of that transaction—would be proxy data. Because forensic science demonstrates associations between people, places, and things through the analysis of proxy data, essentially *all evidence is transfer evidence.* The table below lists some examples in support of this concept.

How much of a material actually transfers from a source to a target depends on a variety of conditions. (In the context of transfer evidence a "target" is simply the location where a bit of transferred evidence ends up.) The conditions that affect transfer include the following points:

- the pressure applied during contact

- the number of contacts (six contacts between two objects should result in more transferred material than one contact, for example)

EXAMPLES OF TRANSFER EVIDENCE

Item	Transferred *From* (source)	Transferred *To* (target/location)
Drugs	dealer	buyer's pocket or car
Blood	victim's body	bedroom wall
Alcohol	glass	drunk driver's bloodstream
Semen	assailant	victim
Ink	writer's pen	stolen check
Handwriting	writer's hand/brain	falsified document
Fibers	kidnapper's car	victim's jacket
Paint chips/smear	vehicle	hit-and-run victim
Bullet	shooter's gun	victim's body
Striations	barrel of shooter's gun	discharged bullet
Imperfections	barrel-cutting tool	shooter's gun's barrel

Note: All evidence in essence is transfer evidence in that it has a source and moves or is moved from that source to a target/location. There are various levels of evidence from the fundamental (striations on the barrel-cutting tool) to the specific (the bullet in the victim's body identified by the striations).

- how easily the item transfers material (mud transfers more readily than does concrete)

- the form of the evidence (solid/particulate, liquid, or gas/aerosol)

- how much of the item is involved in the contact (a square inch should transfer less than a square yard of the same material).

Evidence that is transferred from a source to a target with no intermediaries is said have undergone direct transfer; it has transferred from A to B. Indirect transfer involves one or more intermediate objects—the evidence transfers from A to C to B.

Indirect transfer can become complicated and poses potential limits on interpretation. For example, a person owns two dogs and before he goes to work in the morning each day he pets and scratches them. Later at work, he sits at his desk and talks on the phone. He leaves to get a cup of coffee. When he comes back, a colleague is sitting his desk chair waiting to tell him some news. The dog owner has experienced a direct transfer of his dogs' hairs from them to his pants. His chair, however, has received an indirect transfer of his dogs' hairs—his dogs have never sat in his office desk chair! The colleague who sat in his chair has also experienced an indirect transfer of anything on the chair, except for any fibers originating from the chair's upholstery (a direct transfer). How would he interpret finding his dogs' hairs on his colleague if he didn't know she had sat in his chair? Clearly, while direct transfer may be straightforward to interpret, indirect transfers can be complicated and potentially misleading. It may be more accurate to speak of direct and indirect sources—referring to whether the originating source of the evidence is the transferring item—but the "transfer" terminology has stuck.

The second part of the transfer process is persistence. Once the evidence transfers, it will remain, or persist, in that location until it further transfers (and, potentially, is lost), degrades until it is unusable or unrecognizable, or is collected as evidence. How long evidence persists depends on the following:

- what the evidence is (such as hairs, blood, tool marks, and accelerants)

- the location of the evidence

- the environment around the evidence

- the time from transfer to collection

- "activity" of or around the evidence location

For example, numerous fiber transfer studies demonstrate that 80 percent of the transferred fibers are lost from the time of transfer with normal activity after a period of about four hours. Transfer and persistence studies with other evidence types have shown a similar loss rate.

THE UNIQUENESS OF IDENTITY, CLASS, AND INDIVIDUALIZATION

All objects are unique in space and time. No two (or more) objects are absolutely identical. Take, for example, a mass-produced product like a sneaker. Thousands of sneakers of a particular type may be produced within a year. The manufacturer's goal, to help sell more shoes, is to make them all look and perform the same—consumers demand consistency. This is a help and a hindrance to forensic scientists because it makes it easy to separate one item from another (this red tennis shoe is different from this white one), but these same characteristics make it difficult to separate items with many of the same characteristics (two red tennis shoes). Think about two white sneakers that come off the production line one after the next—how would anyone tell them apart? A person might say, "this one" and "that one," but if the shoes were mixed up, probably no one could sort them again. Some kind of label would have to be added, like numbering them "1" and "2."

Now consider two sneakers that are the same except for color: One is white and one is red. Of course one could tell them apart, but do they belong in the same category? Compared with a brown dress shoe, the two sneakers would have more in common with each other than with the dress shoe. All of the shoes are more alike than any of them are compared with, say, a baseball bat. Forensic scientists have developed terminology to clarify the way they communicate about these issues.

Identification is the examination of the chemical and physical properties of an object and using them to categorize the object as a member of a group. The goal of identification is to answer questions such as: What is the object made of? What is its color, mass, and volume? For example, examining a white powder, performing one or two analyses, and concluding it is cocaine is identification. Determining that a small colored chip is automotive paint is identification. Looking at debris from a crime scene and deciding it contains hairs from a black Labrador retriever is identification (of those hairs).

All the characteristics used to identify an object help to refine that object's identity and its membership in various groups. For example, the debris just described has fibrous objects in it, and that restricts what they could be—most likely hairs or fibers rather than bullets, to use an absurd example. The microscopic characteristics indicate that some of the fibrous objects are hairs, that they are from a dog, and that the hairs are most like those from a specific breed of dog. This description places the hairs into a group of objects with similar characteristics, called a class. All black Labrador retriever hairs would fall into a class; these belong to a larger class of items called dog hairs. Further, all dog hairs can be included in the class of nonhuman hairs and, ultimately, into a more inclusive class called hairs. Going in the other direction, as the process of identification of evidence becomes more specific it permits the analyst to classify the evidence into successively smaller classes of objects.

Class is a moveable definition—it may not be necessary to classify the evidence beyond dog hairs because you are looking for human hairs or textile fibers. Although it is possible to define the dog hairs more completely, the person examining them may not need to do so in the case at hand. Multiple items can be classified differently, depending on what questions need to be asked. For example, an orange, an apple, a bowling ball, a bowling pin, and a banana could be classified by fruit versus non-fruit, round things versus non-round things, and organic versus inorganic. Note that the bowling pin does not fit into either of the classes in the last example because it is made of wood (which is organic) but is covered in paint (which has inorganic components).

Stating that two objects share a class identity may indicate they come from a common source. What is meant by a "common source" depends

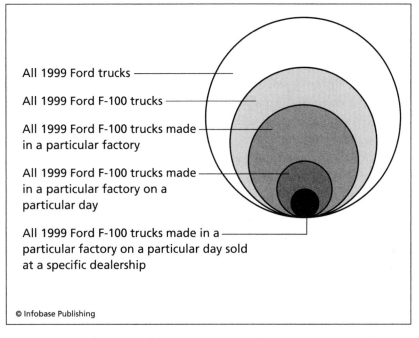

All 1999 Ford trucks

All 1999 Ford F-100 trucks

All 1999 Ford F-100 trucks made in a particular factory

All 1999 Ford F-100 trucks made in a particular factory on a particular day

All 1999 Ford F-100 trucks made in a particular factory on a particular day sold at a specific dealership

Classes are movable and scalable. A class with only one member (one's blue pickup truck) is individualized evidence.

on the material in question, the mode of production, and the specificity of the examinations used to classify the object. A couple of examples should demonstrate the potential complexity of what constitutes a common source. Going back to the two white tennis shoes, what is their common source—the factory, the owner, or where they are found? Because shoes come in pairs, finding one at a crime scene and another in the suspect's apartment could be considered useful to the investigation. The forensic examinations would look for characteristics to determine if the same person (the "common source") owned the two shoes. If the question centered on identifying the production source of the shoes, then the factory would be the "common source."

Another example is fibers that are found on a body left in a ditch, which are determined to be from an automobile. A suspect is developed, and fibers from his car are found to be analytically indistinguishable in all tested traits from the crime scene fibers. Is the suspect's car the common source? For investigative and legal purposes, the car should be considered as such. But certainly it is not the only car with that carpeting—other models from that car manufacturer or even cars made by other manufacturers may have used that carpeting, and the carpeting may not be the only product with those fibers. But given the context of the case, it may be reasonable to conclude that the most logical source for the fibers is the suspect's car. If no suspect was developed, part of the investigation might be to determine who made the fibers and to track what products those fibers went into in an effort to find someone who owns one of those products. In that instance, the common source could be the fiber manufacturer, the carpet manufacturer, or a potential suspect's car, depending on what question is being asked.

If an object can be classified into a group with only one member (itself), it has been individualized. The individualized object has been associated with one, and only one, source: It is unique. The traits that allow for individualization depend in large part but not exclusively on the raw materials, manufacturing methods, and history of use. Sometimes, sufficiently increasing class traits can lead towards individualization; for example, "Trace Evidence in Crime Reconstruction," John Thornton's 2006 article on the classification of firearms evidence, is an excellent, if overlooked, treatment of this issue.

THE CAREFUL INDIVIDUALIZATION OF EVIDENCE

To individualize evidence means to be able to put it into a class with one member. It is the logical extension of the classification of evidence discussed in the previous section. If a forensic scientist can discover properties (normally physical properties) of two pieces of evidence that are unique—that is, properties that are not possessed by any other members of the class of similar materials—then the evidence is said to have been individualized. One example is a broken windowpane in a burglary case: If the fragments of glass found at the crime scene can fit and interlock with a piece of glass found in the suspected burglar's tool kit, for example, then it is reasonable to conclude that those pieces of glass were previously one continuous pane of glass.

This conclusion implies that there is no other piece of glass in the entire world that the fragments under analysis could have come from.

Obviously, no one has tested these pieces of glass against all of the other, similar broken windows to see if they could fit. But to assume uniqueness is not necessarily an error of logic.

Suppose someone took 100 panes of the same type of window glass and broke them. Common sense and experience dictate that each windowpane would break into fragments of different sizes and shapes; in fact, it would not be reasonable to predict or assume that two breakings would yield exactly the same number and shape of broken pieces. The many variables involved—such as the force of the blow, the thickness of the window, the microstructure of the glass, the chemical nature of the material, and the direction of the blow—cannot be exactly duplicated. Therefore, the number and shapes of the fragments produced are essentially random. The probability of two (or more) breaks exactly duplicating the number and shape of fragments is unknown but generally considered to be zero.

REAL EVIDENCE: KNOWN ITEMS AND QUESTIONED ITEMS

Known items and questioned items are both types of real evidence. What distinguishes them from each other is context. The following example illustrates the issue.

Suppose that a motorist strikes and kills a pedestrian with his car and then flees the scene in the vehicle. When the police examines the pedestrian's clothing, minute flakes and smears of paint are found to be embedded in the fabric. Investigators locate and impound the suspect's automobile, and examination of the car reveals fibers embedded in an area that clearly was damaged recently.

How would this evidence be classified? The paint on the victim's coat is questioned evidence because investigators do not know the original source of the paint. Likewise, the fibers found on the damaged area of the car are also questioned items. The co-location of the fibers and damaged area and the wounds/damage and paint smears are indicative of recent contact. In the lab, the paint on the clothing will be compared with paint from the car; this is a known sample because it is known where the sample originated. When the fibers from the car are analyzed, representative fibers from the clothing will be collected for comparison, which makes them known items as well. Thus, the coat and the car are sources of both kinds of items, which allows for their re-association, but it is their context that makes them questioned or known.

Back at the scene where the body was found there are some pieces of yellow, hard, irregularly shaped material. In the lab, the forensic scientist examines this debris and determines that it is plastic, rather than glass; specifically, it is polypropylene. The material found at the scene has now been put in the class of substances that are yellow and made of polypropylene plastic. Further testing may reveal the density, refractive index, hardness, and exact chemical composition of the plastic. This process puts the material into successively smaller classes. That is, it is not just yellow polypropylene plastic, but pieces with a certain shape, refractive index, density, hardness, and so on. In many cases this may be all that is possible with such evidence: Investigators are unable to determine the exact source of the evidence but know only that it could have come from any of a number of places where this material is used—class evidence.

Suppose that the car that is suspected to have been involved in the hit-and-run has a turn-signal lens that is broken and missing some of its plastic. The pieces collected at the scene, however, are too small and the edges too indefinite for a physical match. Pieces of the plastic from the suspect's car can be tested to determine if it has the same physical and chemical characteristics as the plastic found at the crime scene (color, chemical composition, refractive index, and so on). If so, investigators could say that the plastic found at the scene could have come from that broken lens. This is still class evidence, however, because there is nothing unique about these properties; many other cars have similar plastic turn-signal lenses.

Classes are defined by the number and kind of characteristics used to describe them. As an example, think of the vehicle described in the fictitious hit-and-run case. Up until this point, it has been referred to as a car. But what if it were a pickup truck—how would that change things?

Even within the class of pickup trucks, differences can easily be drawn based only on manufacturing locations and days. Following this scheme, the number of trucks could be narrowed down to a very few sold at a particular dealership on a particular day. Classes can be scaled and are context-dependent.

THE RELATIONSHIP AND CONTEXT OF EVIDENCE WITHIN A CRIME SCENE

The relationships between the people, places, and objects involved in crimes are critical to deciding what to examine and how to interpret the results. Consider the evidence associated with an assault. If a sexual

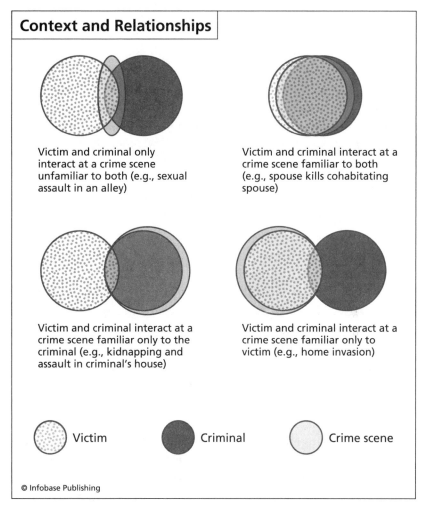

Context and Relationships

Victim and criminal only interact at a crime scene unfamiliar to both (e.g., sexual assault in an alley)

Victim and criminal interact at a crime scene familiar to both (e.g., spouse kills cohabitating spouse)

Victim and criminal interact at a crime scene familiar only to the criminal (e.g., kidnapping and assault in criminal's house)

Victim and criminal interact at a crime scene familiar only to victim (e.g., home invasion)

Victim   Criminal   Crime scene

© Infobase Publishing

The relationships between people, places, and things change the meaningfulness of evidence. Finding a wife's hair on her husband's clothing when they both share the same living space is not forensically useful—that relationship is known to exist. Finding those hairs somewhere unexpected, say, on the trunk latch of the husband's car, might be.

assault occurs and the perpetrator and victim are strangers, more evidence may be relevant than if they lived together or were sexual partners. Strangers are not expected to have met before, and they therefore would not have transferred evidence before the crime. People who live together would have had some opportunities to transfer certain types of evidence (head hairs and carpet fibers from the living room, for example) but not others (semen or vaginal secretions). Spouses or sexual partners, who share the most intimate relationship of the three examples, would share a good deal more information with the victim.

Stranger-on-stranger crimes raise the question of coincidental associations—that is, whether two things that have never been in contact with each other can both exhibit qualities that are analytically indistinguishable at a certain class level. Attorneys will often raise this issue during a cross-examination—"Couldn't [insert evidence type here] really have come from *anywhere*? Aren't [generic class level evidence] very *common*?"

It is true that some kinds of evidence are either quite common, such as white cotton fibers, or have few distinguishing characteristics, such as indigo-dyed cotton from denim fabric. But it has been proven for a wide variety of evidence that coincidental matches are extremely rare. The variety of mass-produced goods, consumer choices, economic factors, and other product traits create a nearly infinite combination of comparable characteristics for the items involved in any given situation. And in a particular context, even commonplace materials can be important. In a hit-and-run case, for example, finding blue denim fibers in the grille of the car involved may be significant if the victim was wearing blue jeans (or khakis!).

It is important to establish the context of the crime and those involved early in the investigation. This sets the stage for what evidence is significant, what methods may be most effective for collection or analysis, and what may be safely ignored. Using context for direction prevents the indiscriminate collection of items that clog the workflow of the forensic science laboratory. Every item collected must be transferred to the laboratory and—at a minimum—cataloged, and this takes people and time. Evidence collection based on intelligent decision-making, instead of fear of missing something, produces a better result in the laboratory and the courts.

COMPARISON OF EVIDENCE

There are two processes in the analysis of evidence. The first has already been discussed: identification. Recall that identification is the process of discovering physical and chemical characteristics of evidence with an eye toward putting the evidence into progressively smaller classes. The second process is comparison. Comparison is an attempt to discover the source of evidence and its degree of relatedness to the questioned material. The questioned evidence is compared with objects whose source is known. The goal is to determine whether there are sufficient common physical and/or chemical characteristics between the samples. If so, it can be concluded that an association exists between the questioned and known items.

An association can be described as a relationship between one or more items of evidence and a putative source. The strength of any association depends upon a number of factors, including:

- the kind of evidence under examination
- variation within and between samples
- the amount of evidence
- the location of evidence
- transfer and cross-transfer
- the number of different kinds of evidence associated to one or more sources

Individualization occurs when at least one unique characteristic is found to exist in both the known and the questioned samples. Although identification can significantly reduce the number of items in the class that evidence belongs to, individualization cannot be accomplished by identification alone.

Finding similarities is not enough, however. It is very important that no significant differences exist between the questioned and known items. This relates to the central idea of going from general to specific in comparison—any significant difference should stop the comparison process in its tracks. What is a significant difference? The principal example is a class characteristic that is *not* shared between the questioned and known items, such as tread design on shoes or shade differences in fiber color. Sometimes the disparity is small, such as a few millimeters' difference in fiber diameter, or distinct, like the cross-sectional shape of fibers or hair color. In any case, a significant difference indicates that the questioned and known evidence are not related.

DEVELOPMENT OF THE SCIENTIFIC METHOD

Science is a way of examining the world and discovering it. The process of science, the scientific method, is to propose and refine plausible explanations about any unknown situation. It involves asking and answering questions in a formal way and then drawing conclusions from the answers.

Science, through its method, has two hallmarks. The first is that the questions that are asked must be testable. For instance, it is not scientific to ask "How many angels can dance on the head of a pin?" or "Why do ghosts haunt this house?" because a test cannot be constructed to answer either of these questions. The second hallmark of science is repeatability. Science is a public endeavor, and its results are published for many reasons, the most important of which is for other scientists to review the work and determine if it is sound. If nobody but one person can make a particular experiment work, it is not science. Other testers must be able to take the same kind of samples and methods, repeat the original experiments, and get the same results for it to be science.

Interestingly, an important person in the history of science was not even a scientist at all, but a lawyer. Sir Francis Bacon, who rose to be Lord Chancellor of England during the reign of James I, wrote a famous (and his greatest) book called *Novum Organum*. In it, Bacon put forth the first theory of the scientific method: The scientist should be a disinterested observer of the world with a clear mind, unbiased by preconceptions that might influence the scientist's understanding. Such a misunderstanding might cause error to infiltrate the scientific data. Given enough observations, patterns of data will emerge, allowing scientists to make both specific statements and generalizations about nature.

This theory sounds pretty straightforward. But it is wrong. All serious scientific thinkers and philosophers have rejected Bacon's idea that science works through the collection of unbiased observations. Everything about the way people do science, from the words to the instrumentation to the procedures, depends on individuals' preconceived ideas and experience about how the world works. It is impossible to make observations about the world without knowing what is worth observing and what is not worth observing. One is constantly filtering experiences and observations about the world through those things already experienced. Objectivity is impossible for people to achieve.

Another important person in the philosophy of science, Sir Karl Popper, proposed that all science begins with a prejudice, a theory, a hypothesis—in short, an idea with a specific viewpoint. Popper worked from the premise that a theory can never be proved by agreement with observation, but it can be proved wrong by disagreement. The asymmetric, or one-sided, nature of science makes it unique among ways of knowing about the world: Good ideas can be proven wrong to make way for even better ideas. Popper coined this aspect of science "falsificationism," the idea that a proper scientific statement must be able to be proven false. Popper's view of constant testing to disprove statements biased by the preconceived notions of scientists replaced Bacon's view of the disinterested observer.

But Popper's ideas do not accurately describe science. While it may be impossible to prove a theory true, it is almost as difficult to prove one false by Popper's methods. The trouble lies in distilling a falsifiable statement from a theory. To do so, one must almost always make additional assumptions that are not covered by the idea or theory itself. If the statement is shown to be false, the tester does not know if it was one of the other assumptions or the theory itself that is at fault. This confuses the issue and clouds what the scientist thinks she has discovered.

Clearly, defining science is difficult. It takes a great deal of hard work to develop a new theory that agrees with the entirety of what is known in any area of science. Popper's idea about falsifiability, that scientists attack a theory at its weakest point, is simply not the way people explore the world. To show that a theory is wrong or to develop a new theory in any modern science by trying to prove every single assumption inherent in the theory false would take too much time, too many resources, and too many people. It would be impossible!

Thomas Kuhn, a physicist by education and training who later became a historian and philosopher of science, offered a new way of thinking about science. Kuhn wrote that science involves paradigms, which are a consensual understanding of how the world works. Within a given paradigm, scientists add information, ideas, and methods that steadily accumulate and reinforce their understanding of the world. This Kuhn called "normal science."

With time, according to Kuhn, scientists encounter contradictions and observations that are difficult to explain and that cannot be dealt with under the current paradigm. These difficulties are set aside to be dealt with later, so as not to endanger the status quo of the paradigm. Eventually, enough of these difficulties accumulate and the paradigm can no longer be supported. When this happens, Kuhn maintains, a scientific revolution ensues that dismantles the old paradigm and replaces it with a new paradigm.

Kuhn's main point is that while key aspects of theories are tested— and some are falsified—the daily business of science is not to overturn its core ideas regularly. Falsifiability is not the only criterion for what science is. If a theory makes novel and unexpected predictions, and those predictions are verified by experiments that reveal new and useful or interesting phenomena, then the chances that the theory is correct are greatly enhanced. However, science does undergo startling changes of perspective that lead to new and, invariably, better ways of understanding the world. Thus, although science does not proceed smoothly and incrementally, it is one of the few areas of human endeavor that are truly progressive. The scientific debate is very different from what happens in a court of law, but just as in the law, it is crucial that every idea receive the most vigorous possible advocacy, just in case it might be right.

USING THE SCIENTIFIC METHOD ON TRACE EVIDENCE

In the language of science, the particular questions to be tested are called hypotheses. Forensic scientists develop and test hypotheses as part of their daily work. Suppose, for example, that hairs are found on the bed where a victim has been sexually assaulted. Are the hairs those of the victim, the suspect, or someone else? The forensic scientists would begin by translating this question into a hypothesis, which

Sir Karl Popper (1902-1994): Political Philosopher

Karl Raimund Popper is regarded as one of the greatest philosophers of science in the 20th century as well as a noted social philosopher, a self-professed "critical-rationalist," and an opponent of skepticism, conventionalism, and relativism in science. Born in Vienna on July 28, 1902, Popper was educated at the University of Vienna where he received a Ph.D. in philosophy in 1928, and then taught mathematics and physics at secondary school until 1936. In 1937, the rise of Nazism motivated Popper to emigrate to New Zealand, where he became a lecturer in philosophy at the University of Canterbury. In 1946, he moved to England to teach at the London School of Economics, and in 1949 became professor of logic and scientific method at the University of London. In 1965 he was knighted by Queen Elizabeth II and later elected a Fellow of the Royal Society. He retired from academic life in 1969, though he remained intellectually active until his death in 1994.

In 1934, he published his first book, *Logik der Forschung (The Logic of Scientific Discovery),* in which he attacked induction (a mode of reasoning that heralds the universal from the particular, with remarks such as "I've only ever seen black ravens, so all ravens must be black") and developed the theory of falsificationism, the idea that science advances by unjustified, exaggerated guesses followed by criticism. Only a hypothesis that is capable of clashing with an observation report is allowed to be considered as scientific.

Popper argued that scientific theories are essentially abstract and therefore can only be tested indirectly. A scientific theory can never logically be proven by any number of positive or negative experimental outcomes. One counterexample can destroy a theory's validity, thereby rendering it and any implications derived from it as false. Popper's account of the logical asymmetry between verification and falsificationism lies at the heart of his philosophy of science. Falsificationism became Popper's only criterion of demarcation between what is and is not genuinely scientific: A theory should be considered scientific if and only if it is falsifiable. The more a theory is supported, the more useful it becomes

(continues)

(continued)

for explaining things. Robust theories survive longer. Rigorous testing, however, does not insure a scientific theory from future refutation.

Popper has his critics. The Quine-Duhem thesis, for example, argues that, because each theory is made up of a chain of incompletely identified assumptions, testing a single hypothesis on its own is impossible. Either the whole collection of theories has been collectively falsified or supported; if falsified, the element(s) responsible cannot be conclusively identified and singled out. Another objection is that it is not always clear that when evidence contradicts a hypothesis whether the fault lies with the hypothesis or the evidence. Sorting faulty evidence from faulty hypotheses needs to be done in each individual case. A challenge to Popper's falsificationism can be raised on the basis of logic. Statements such as "There are black holes," which cannot be falsified by any possible observation, seem to be legitimately scientific. On the other hand, statements such as "For every metal, there is a temperature at which it will melt," leave falsification in murky waters—the statement can neither be confirmed nor falsified by any possible observation.

Falsificationism is one way to describe how theories attain, maintain, and lose scientific status. Therefore, individual consequences of current specific scientific theories are scientific in that they are part of what we know to be scientific knowledge right now. Falsifying a theory may lead to some of its implications being temporarily of uncertain scientific status, but may not render it completely obsolete.

By the time of his death on September 17, 1994, Popper received many awards and honors, including the Lippincott Award of the American Political Science Association, the Sonning Prize, and, from Austria, the Grand Decoration of Honor in Gold.

could be framed as: "There is a significant difference between the questioned hairs and the known hairs from the suspect." Notice that the hypothesis is formed as a neutral statement that can be either proven or disproved.

After the hypothesis has been formed, the forensic scientist seeks to collect data that shed light on the hypothesis. Known hairs from the suspect are compared with those from the scene and the victim. All relevant data will be collected, without regard to whether it favors the hypothesis. Once collected, the data will be carefully examined to determine what value they have in proving or disproving the hypothesis; this is the data's probative value. (The word *probative* means serving to prove.) If the questioned hairs are analytically indistinguishable from the known hairs, then the hypothesis is rejected. The scientist could then conclude that the questioned hairs could have come from the suspect.

Suppose, however, that *most* of the data suggest that the suspect is the one that left the hairs, but there are not enough data to associate the hairs with him. It cannot be said that the hypothesis has been disproved (there are some similarities) but neither can it be said that it has been proved (some differences exist but their significance is uncertain). Although we would like to be able to prove unequivocally that someone is or is not the source of evidence, this is not always possible. As explained previously, not all evidence can be individualized. The important thing to note here is that a forensic scientist conducts evidence analysis by forming many hypotheses and perhaps rejecting some as the investigation progresses.

Some preliminary questions must be answered before one can even begin to formulate hypotheses. If extremely large amounts of material are submitted as evidence, one such question is: How are they sampled? This often happens in drug cases where, for example, a 50-pound (22.7-kg) block of marijuana or several kilograms of cocaine are received in one package. The laboratory must have a protocol for sampling large quantities of material so that the samples taken are representative of the whole. The other situation that involves sampling is cases where there are many exhibits that appear to contain the same thing, for instance, 100 0.5-ounce (14-g) packets of white powder. The laboratory and the scientist must decide how many samples to take and what tests to perform. This is especially important because the results of the analyses will ascribe the characteristics of the samples to the whole exhibit, such as identifying 1,000 packets of powder as 23 percent cocaine based upon analysis of a fraction of the packets.

The opposite situation raises a different preliminary question: Is there sufficient material to analyze? If the amount of the evidence is limited, then the tester has to make choices about which tests to perform and in what order. The general rule is to perform nondestructive tests first, because they conserve material. Most jurisdictions also have evidentiary rules that require that some evidence be set aside for additional analyses by opposing experts; if the entire sample will be consumed in an analysis, then both sides must be informed that not enough evidence will be available to have additional analyses performed.

What happens in cases where more than one kind of analysis must be done on the same item of evidence? Consider a handgun, received into evidence from a shooting incident, with red stains and possible fingerprints on it. These conditions mean that firearms testing, serology, latent fingerprints, and possibly DNA analysis will be performed on the handgun. They should be conducted in an order such that one exam does not preclude or spoil the next. In this case, the order should be first serology (and DNA), then latent print, and finally firearms testing.

It is important to note that one seemingly small piece of evidence can be subjected to many examinations. Take the example of a threatening letter that supposedly contains anthrax or some other contagion. The envelope and the letter could be subjected to the following exams, in the following order:

- disease diagnosis, to determine if they really contain the suspected contagion

- trace evidence analysis, for hairs or fibers in the envelope or stuck to the adhesives (stamp, closure, tape used to seal it)

- DNA analysis, from saliva on the stamp or the envelope closure

- questioned document examination, for the paper, lettering, and other aspects of the form of the letter

- ink analysis, to determine what was used to write the message, address, and the like

- handwriting, typewriter, or printer analysis, as appropriate

- latent fingerprint testing

- content analysis, to evaluate the nature of the writer's intent and other investigative clues

In this example, the order of the exams is crucial to ensure not only the integrity of the evidence, but also the safety of the scientists and their coworkers.

Some evidence, like the traces that might be found on the envelope in the current example, is small and easily overlooked. Other evidence, by contrast, can be very, very large. It is important to realize that *anything* can become evidence. If forensic scientists are to solve the most difficult of crimes, they must keep an open mind.

2

Forensic Applications

The forensic scientist has a formidable arsenal at his command to analyze evidence: some simple, some complex, yet all are powerful. Between spectroscopy, microscopy, and chromatography, there is little that is beyond analysis. Interestingly, chromatography stands alone, as spectroscopy and microscopy (both dealing with light as they do) can be combined in a single instrument to allow the analysis of microscopic evidence.

SPECTROSCOPY

Simply put, spectroscopy is the study of the interaction of matter with electromagnetic energy. Spectroscopy is used routinely in forensic science to characterize molecules, identify them, and compare questioned and known evidence. The way in which atoms and molecules interact with electromagnetic energy, such as light, reveals their structure. The electromagnetic spectrum, the range of energy in the universe, is composed of various regions, each of which can provide different information about the structure of molecules.

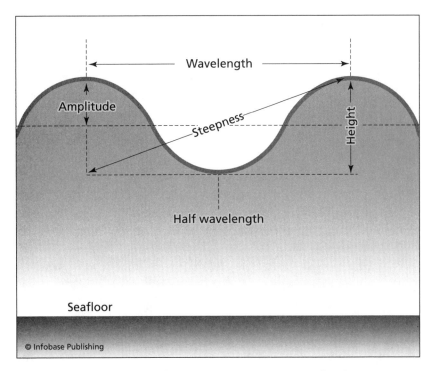

A wavelength is the distance between two waves, measured at the same points on the waves.

Think of the electromagnetic spectrum as a series of waves flowing out of a source in all directions. Each wave has a specific length, noted in equations by the Greek letter lambda (λ). The distance between two waves is measured at the same points on the waves. Electromagnetic radiation can also be described in terms of its frequency (f), which is the number of waves that pass a given point in one second. Frequency is also known as cycles per second or hertz (Hz). Wavelength and frequency are calculated in relation to the speed of light:

$$C = f/\lambda$$

where C is the speed of light. The relationship between wavelength and frequency is inverse; that is, as frequency goes up, wavelength goes down and vice versa.

Another way to express frequency is by wave numbers. A wave number is the inverse of the wavelength measured in centimeters: A wave number is 1 cm^{-1} (reciprocal centimeters). Interestingly, a wavelength can be expressed in any unit of length—millimeters, centimeters, or even meters. The units are chosen depending on which region of the electromagnetic spectrum is of interest in small, whole numbers. For example, in the ultraviolet region, nanometers (nm, 10^{-9} meters) are used to define the range: about 200–350 nanometers. A graph or plot of the energy response at each wavelength of light is called a spectrum (plural, spectra). A spectrum is thus a graphic representation of frequency and intensity for each wavelength.

Physicists also describe light as tiny packets, or quanta (singular, quantum), of energy called photons. Energy is represented by the letter E in equations. The energy of a photon is related to its wavelength (and also its frequency, since these properties are related), as shown in following equations:

$$E = hf$$
$$E = hC/f$$

The h represents Planck's constant, which is used to ensure that the units are the same on both sides of the equation. Planck's constant changes as the units of energy change. The equations show that as the frequency of light goes up, so does its energy, and as the wavelength goes up, the energy goes down.

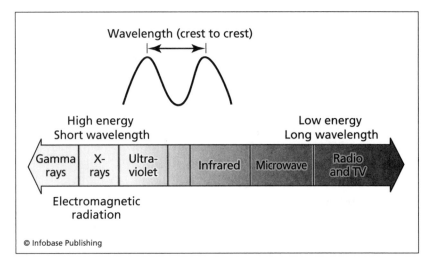

The electromagnetic spectrum is the range of all possible electromagnetic radiation. Many of the ranges of the spectrum are analytically useful in forensic science.

At the far left of this electromagnetic (or EM) spectrum are gamma rays, which are very energetic and can pass through matter. When gamma rays pass through living tissue, they can cause damage or even destroy cells. X-rays, lower in energy, can pass through most objects but are deflected by dense matter, such as metal or bones. On medical X-ray films, these materials appear opaque and other, softer structures can be visualized. Even lower in frequency and energy than X-rays are ultraviolet and visible radiation, which are two of the most useful energy ranges for forensic analysis. The ultraviolet region is so named because it is next to the violet area of the region of visible light (the light that human eyes see as color), and *ultra* means "beyond," so ultraviolet radiation is just beyond the visible region.

Below the red region of visible light is the infrared region (*infra* is Latin for "below"). Infrared radiation is less energetic (has lower frequency and longer wavelength) than ultraviolet and visible radiation. When absorbed by matter, infrared radiation causes the bonds between atoms in a molecule to vibrate like two weights on either end of a spring. The infrared region is also very important in the analysis of trace evidence in forensic science.

Next is the microwave region that causes molecules to rotate or spin, creating friction, which emits heat. Microwave ovens work by this principle: The microwaves are absorbed by water molecules in the food and as they spin, the heat cooks the food. At the lowest end of the spectrum are radio waves, which have large wavelengths and tiny frequencies. Neither microwaves nor radio waves are used in forensic analysis.

Each region of the electromagnetic spectrum has a particular effect on matter; additionally, the different regions of radiation elicit different changes in different materials. How matter interacts with electromagnetic radiation of various frequencies is the basis of spectroscopy. Spectroscopists study the interactions of energy and matter to identify materials and compare them; plots of these interactions are called spectra. These interactions can reveal information about the material under study and can identify the material.

Different methods of spectroscopy yield different information about a molecule. In combination, they can completely describe a molecule through its characteristic features. Typical methods of spectroscopy include mass spectrometry, ultraviolet/visible spectroscopy, fluorescence spectroscopy, infrared spectrometry, and Raman spectroscopy.

INTERACTIONS OF ENERGY AND MATTER

Radiation Range	Molecular Energy Change
ultraviolet / visible	electronic, vibrational, and rotational
infrared	vibrational and rotational
far infrared / microwave	rotational
radio	nuclear spin flips

Note: The energy of the radiation interacting with a material determines the molecular energy change.

Mass spectrometry uses high-energy electrons to ionize molecules. An ion is an atom or molecule that has lost or gained one or more electrons, making it negatively or positively charged. A negatively charged ion, which has more electrons in its electron shells than it has protons in its nuclei, is known as an anion due to its attraction to anodes. A positively charged ion, which has fewer electrons than protons, is known as a cation due to its attraction to cathodes. The mass-to-charge ratio of the resulting ions is measured very accurately by electrostatic acceleration and magnetic field perturbation, providing a precise molecular weight. Ion fragmentation patterns may be related to the structure of the molecular ion.

Ultraviolet/visible (UV/vis, and pronounced "yoo-vee-viz") spectroscopy excites molecules with relatively high-energy light. Some of this excitation is absorbed by the molecule's structure, and the instrument records the pattern of this absorption. A related type of spectroscopy, fluorescence spectroscopy, measures the long-wavelength light emitted by a substance excited by a shorter-wavelength beam.

Infrared (IR) spectroscopy measures the absorption of lower-energy radiation. The IR beam causes vibrational and rotational excitation of groups of atoms within the molecule. Each functional group has a characteristic absorption pattern that is easily identified.

Raman spectroscopy is a technique that measures light scattering. When light is scattered by a molecule, most of the photons are elastically scattered; that is, they have the same energy (frequency) and, therefore, wavelength, as the incoming photons. A small fraction gets scattered at frequencies different from, and usually lower than, the frequency of the incident light. The process leading to this is called the Raman effect. Raman scattering can occur with a change in vibrational, rotational, or electronic energy of a molecule. A plot of intensity of scattered light versus energy difference is a Raman spectrum. Raman spectroscopy is not widely employed in forensic science, but its importance is growing.

The two regions of radiation that are currently most important in characterizing evidence are the ultraviolet/visible (UV/vis) and the infrared (IR) regions.

UV/vis SPECTROSCOPY

All compounds absorb and reflect more or less light of certain wavelengths in the UV/vis range; this is called color. UV/vis spectroscopy measures how much a given material absorbs or reflects ultraviolet and visible radiation. Color is seen only in the visible range of the EM spec-

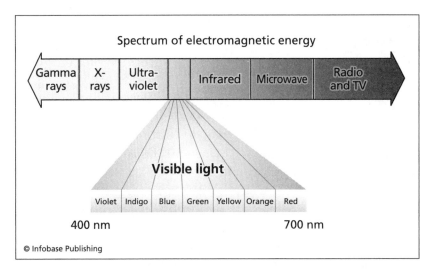

The visible range covers approximately 400 to 700 nanometers of the spectrum. The order of the colors of the visible spectrum, in decreasing wavelength, is red, orange, yellow, green, blue, indigo, and violet.

trum; the human visual system acts like a spectrometer, detecting colors that are transmitted through or reflected off of an object.

Light appears to be uniform but is actually composed of a range of wavelengths. The component colors of the visible portion can be separated by shining white light through a prism, which bends the light according to its wavelength. By convention, visible light is treated as a wave phenomenon and is described by wavelength or frequency. The visible range covers approximately 400 to 800 nanometers of the spectrum. Red is the longest visible wavelength and violet the shortest. (The order of the colors of the visible spectrum, in decreasing wavelength, can be remembered by the "name" Roy G. Biv: red, orange, yellow, green, blue, indigo, and violet.)

Material absorbs or reflects UV/vis radiation depending on how its electrons interact with the radiation. All matter consists of atoms; atoms, in turn, consist of a nucleus, made up of positively charged protons and neutral neutrons, and negatively charged electrons. Electrons inhabit regions called orbitals that exist in approximately concentric spheres around the nucleus of each atom, like the layers of an onion. Neutral atoms have equal numbers of electrons (−) and protons (+); accordingly, they have no net negative or positive charge. When atoms combine to make molecules (the basis of compounds and materials), they either share or donate/accept electrons to form covalent (sharing) or ionic (donating/accepting) bonds. Shared electrons are in the outermost orbital, called the outer shell.

Although outer shell electrons are the least energetic electrons in any given molecule, they can be promoted to a higher energy level (closer to the nucleus) by absorbing energy from the outside. An atom or molecule can only absorb the exact amount (quantum) of energy that corresponds to the difference in energy between the occupied and unoccupied energy levels. Because of this, a molecule can absorb energy and promote an electron only if it encounters a photon of the proper energy quantum. Like rungs on a ladder—a person can be on one rung or the next but cannot be between the rungs—so are the energy states between quanta.

A material exposed to UV/vis radiation will absorb photons of specific wavelengths and particular frequencies. Because the atoms cannot take on all of the energy, some of this radiation is absorbed and some reflected. The portion of the UV/vis radiation that is reflected is what people perceive as color. If the sample compound does not absorb light of a given wavelength, then the intensity coming into the sample (I) is equal to the intensity coming out (I_O), or

$$I = I_O$$

If the sample compound does absorb light, however, then I is less than I_O, and a spectrometer can plot this intensity difference on a graph, as a spectrum. The intensity difference may be expressed in terms of either the amount transmitted (*transmittance*, or *T*), where $T = I/I_O$, or the amount absorbed (*absorbance*, or *A*), where $A = \log I_O/I$. Logically, if no absorption has occurred, $T = 1.0$ and $A = 0$.

Most spectrometers display absorbance on the vertical axis, and the observed range is from 0 (100 percent transmittance) to 2 (1 percent transmittance). The wavelength of maximum absorbance is a characteristic value, designated as λ_{max} (pronounced "lambda max"). Different compounds may have very different absorption maxima (the plural of maximum) and absorbances.

A UV/vis spectrum tends to have only a few broad peaks. This is indicative of the way UV/vis radiation is absorbed because very few electrons can be promoted or exchanged in the average molecule. Additionally, in the UV/vis range, few wavelengths exist where a useful number of photons will be absorbed. The peaks, and therefore the spectra, are vague and this limits their usefulness: UV/vis spectra are not typically useful for identification of questioned substances. The typical UV/vis range spectrum is not sufficiently distinctive to allow unique identification a substance from all other similar substances. But, because of the range of colors in the UV/vis range, colored substances, like fibers, can be compared readily. A wide variety of colors are possible in textiles and many chemicals can be used to produce those colors.

Most but not all materials absorb UV/vis radiation; those that do have "submolecules," or groups, called chromophores. Chromophores absorb UV/vis radiation at certain wavelengths but not at others. For example, if a substance absorbs energies except those in the blue range of the visible spectrum, the substance will appear blue. The absorbance spectrum will show how the absorption of the light energies will depend upon the wavelength of light—high absorbance, high peaks. In transmittance, the opposite will be true. Some chromophores will absorb strongly or weakly, depending on their size and structure (number of electrons that they can share, donate, or accept). The magnitude of λ reflects both the size of the chromophore and the probability that light of a given wavelength will be absorbed when it strikes the chromophore.

UV/vis spectra are collected by a spectrophotometer. The spectrophotometer is an instrument that detects and analyzes radiation in the UV/vis range; spectrometers for other electromagnetic ranges are also available. A beam of light from a source that emits radiation in specific range—the entire UV/vis range, from 300–800 nanometers—is separated into its component wavelengths by a prism or diffraction grating (a filter that separates light like a prism). Each single-wavelength (monochromatic) beam is split into two equal-intensity beams of the same wavelength. One beam passes through the sample being analyzed; this is called the sample beam. The other beam, the reference beam, passes through the system without touching the sample. The intensities of the two light beams are then measured by electronic detectors and compared. The intensity of the reference beam, which should have suffered little or no light absorption, is defined as I_O. The intensity of the sample beam is defined as I. Because of computerized equipment and high-speed detectors, collecting a spectrum takes only seconds. The speed and accuracy of modern spectrometers have made UV/vis spectroscopy a very useful method for characterizing forensic evidence.

INFRARED SPECTROPHOTOMETRY

The infrared range of radiation induces vibrations at the molecular level and infrared spectroscopy analyzes these vibrations to provide structural information about the material. Infrared spectroscopy works much like harmonic motion—that is, sound. An easy conceptual model to understand infrared spectroscopy is to imagine two balls connected with a spring, called a simple harmonic oscillator. A ball on the spring will vibrate back and forth (oscillate) at a certain frequency, depending on the force applied, the ball's mass, and the stiffness of the spring: A ball with a low mass is lighter and will move more easily than one with a high mass. These rules determine this oscillation frequency as follows:

- lower masses oscillate at a higher frequency than higher masses

- very stiff springs bend with more difficulty and return to their original shape more quickly

- weak springs are easily bent and take longer to return to their original shape

- thus, stiffer springs oscillate at higher frequencies than weak ones

The balls and spring are like a chemical bond between two atoms—the bond is the spring and the two atoms (or groups of atoms) are the balls. The atoms, therefore, act like simple harmonic oscillators. Every atom has a different mass and the various bonds (single, double, and triple) between them all have different degrees of stiffness. Each kind of molecule, because it is a combination of atoms and bonds, vibrates at its own specific frequency. As an example, imagine a violin. If the E string is plucked, it will vibrate at the frequency that sounds the E note. If another string is plucked, the E string might also vibrate because some of energy from the vibrating string was transferred to the E string, causing it to vibrate as well. When a molecule vibrates at a certain frequency and encounters another vibration of *exactly* the same frequency, the oscillator will absorb that energy.

All the simple harmonic oscillators in molecules vibrate somewhat all the time. Infrared light vibrates in the same frequency range as the vibrating molecules. The portion of the infrared region most useful for analysis of organic compounds has a wavelength range from 2,500 to 16,000 nanometers, with a corresponding frequency range from 1.9×10^{13} to 1.2×10^{14} Hz. If a molecule encounters infrared light, the harmonic oscillators in the molecule absorb those same frequencies in the infrared light exactly matching their own. By absorbing the energy of the infrared light, their amplitude increases and the bonds (springs) stretch farther. The energy that is not absorbed passes through the material (transmitted). Molecules experience a variety of vibrational responses (back and forth, stretches, rotation, etc.). Infrared spectrometers permit chemists to record the absorption spectra of compounds, and these spectra reflect the compounds' molecular structure.

Each different chemical bond in the molecule has its own characteristic vibrations, and each bond can undergo a number of different kinds

Fourier Transformation in Infrared Spectroscopy

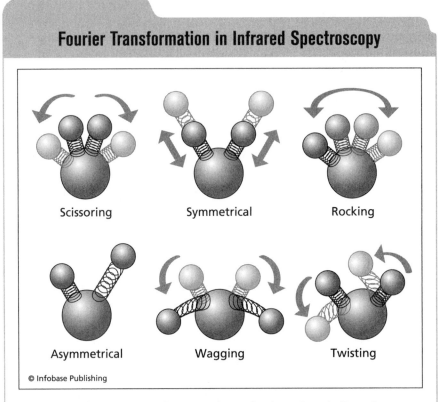

Scissoring   Symmetrical   Rocking

Asymmetrical   Wagging   Twisting

© Infobase Publishing

A molecular vibration occurs when atoms in a molecule are in periodic motion while the molecule as a whole has constant translational and rotational motion. The frequency of the periodic motion is known as a vibration frequency.

Molecular vibrations are a type of signal, and any signal can be described in either time or frequency. Data are most commonly measured in terms of time (the "time domain"), such as a person's heart rate tracked on a piece of hospital equipment or automobile signals tracked an oscilloscope at a local mechanic shop. On a graph of these measurements, the vertical dimension is the signal's amplitude and the horizontal dimension is time. The "frequency domain" is like the heartbeats per minute being lined up along an axis, with the number of beats stacked up like a bar graph. But the transformation can get a little complicated. The input signal must be separated into many simpler signals, and then the system or instrument must be trained how to respond to the incoming signal. Today, this is accomplished by an algorithm called the Fourier transform.

As already mentioned, the portion of the infrared spectrum most useful for analysis of organic compounds ranges in wavelength from 2,500 to 16,000 nanometers and ranges in frequency from 1.9×10^{13} to 1.2×10^{14} Hz. From the perspective of analysis, this is a broad range. Traditional IR instruments took quite a long time to scan every frequency in the IR portion of the spectrum. The instrument had to measure the absorption at frequency #1 (and measure it multiple times to reduce error) and then "move" to frequency #2, and so on. With the advent of the Fourier transform algorithm, infrared spectroscopy became faster, more reliable, and a mainstay of chemistry laboratories around the world.

The Fourier transform was developed by the French mathematician Baron Jean-Baptiste-Joseph Fourier (1768–1830) around 1810, while he was researching the conduction of heat. The Fourier transform is important because it can relate numerous physical variables, like time and frequency. Fourier transform spectroscopy (FTS) became practical in the early 1950s, when research groups assembled and tested high-resolution spectrometers, demonstrating that certain theoretical advantages could be achieved. During the 1950s and 1960s, despite advances in the laboratory, the development of FTS was limited by the high cost and computational power of computers.

An algorithm known as the fast Fourier transform (FFT) algorithm, allows for a quick computation, converting frequency to space. This provides for a quicker analysis time. The FFT reduced the computation time by several orders of magnitude and made transforming large spectra feasible. The FFT algorithm appears below:

$$F(v) = \int\infty/-\infty\ f(t)e^{-i(2\Pi)vt}\ dt$$

and

$$f(t) = \int\infty/-\infty\ 2\Pi\ F(v)\ e^{i(2\Pi)vt}\ dt$$

(continues)

(continued)

Today, commercial Fourier transform spectrometers are the norm in many applications. Many spectroscopic techniques have benefited by the application of the Fourier algorithm, such as Fourier transform Raman spectroscopy, Fourier transform microwave spectroscopy, and Fourier transform nuclear magnetic resonance spectroscopy.

The basic infrared spectrophotometer is somewhat similar in appearance to the UV/vis spectrophotometer. Modern infrared instruments are based on somewhat different principles (which are beyond the scope of this book), but the results are the same as with basic instruments. Detectors are also different from those used in UV/vis spectrophotometry. Infrared detectors are usually some type of thermocouple—a device that converts heat into electricity. To increase the sensitivity of these detectors, they are often housed in a flask that has liquid nitrogen circulating around it to make it very cold. Spectrometry is one of the most widely used techniques in forensic science, but without the development of the Fourier transform algorithm none of it would be possible.

of vibrations. However, unlike UV/vis absorptions, there are many infrared absorptions in each type of molecule. Remembering the example of the E string on the violin, imagine hearing, but not seeing, someone strum a stringed instrument. A violin sounds very different than a harp does. Similarly, the multiple vibrations of a molecule create a pattern of response that identifies the vibrations and, thus, the material. Even the slightest change in the composition of a molecule will result in a different infrared spectrum. The infrared spectrum of a substance is unique and can thus be used to unequivocally identify that substance. Infrared spectrophotometry is one of the two analytical techniques (the other being gas chromatography–mass spectrometry) that can be used for identification of substances, such as drugs.

None of the spectroscopic methods discussed so far in this chapter are designed to accept a microscopic sample. Suppose a forensic scientist receives individual colored fibers as evidence and wants to collect both their visible spectra (to compare their colors) and their infrared spectra (to identify them chemically). How is the desired information to be collected? To analyze such samples, a microscope can be joined with a spectrophotometer to make a microspectrophotometer. A microspectrophotometer can be thought of as a microscope, a light source, a monochromator, and a detector. There are microspectrophotometers for visible and UV light, and for the infrared region. The object, a fiber in this case, is mounted on the stage of the microscope, and all of the light is focused on the object. The detector detects the light transmitted by the object. Much of what a forensic scientist analyzes is microscopic and the addition of the microscope to the analytical spectrometers discussed so far is invaluable to the analysis of trace evidence.

MICROSCOPY

The very nature of trace evidence means that what is being examined is small; microscopic, in fact. After visually examining the evidence grossly (which means with an unaided eye), the next step is to examine it with some type of microscope. The microscope is a nearly universal symbol of science, and most people think of forensic science as well when they see one—microscopes appear in Sir Arthur Conan Doyle's Sherlock Holmes stories, showing the great detective examining bits of evidence through a microscope. The microscope may seem to be a relic suitable only for museums or beginning science classes compared with today's advanced instrumentation. The microscope is central, however, to nearly every examination in trace evidence. Experts such as the renowned Dr. Walter McCrone, have shown that microscopy is applicable to every area of forensic science (and others sciences as well). Microscopy can be as powerful as many current technologies and, in some cases, more powerful, but the equipment costs a fraction of larger, computerized instruments. For example, microscopy can easily distinguish between cotton and rayon textile fibers; to an infrared spectrometer, they both appear to be cellulose.

Forensic microscopy is more than simply looking at small things. Attorneys may challenge a trace scientist in court by asking, "All you do is just look at these things, isn't that correct?" and nothing could be

Walter McCrone (1916–2002): A Preeminent Microscopist

Dr. Walter Cox McCrone was an American chemist who was considered one of the leading experts in microscopy. McCrone received a bachelor's degree in chemistry from Cornell University in 1938 and a Ph.D. in organic chemistry from the same institution in 1942. He became a microscopist and materials scientist at the Armour Research Foundation (now the Illinois Institute of Technology) from 1944 to 1956 after a two-year postdoctoral position at Cornell. McCrone left his job in 1956 to become an independent consultant. In 1960, he founded McCrone Associates (part of the McCrone Group), an analytical consulting firm in Chicago (now located in Westmont, Illinois). That same year, he founded the McCrone Research Institute, a nonprofit organization for teaching and research in microscopy and crystallography. Since then, the McCrone Research Institute has taught more than 25,000 students in all facets of microscopy. The institute remains a leading educational facility within the world of microscopy. In the 1990s, Dr. McCrone and his wife Lucy endowed a chair of chemical microscopy in the College of Arts and Sciences at Cornell. Named the Emile M. Chamot Professorship in Chemistry, it honors Emile Monnin Chamot, a Cornell professor of chemical microscopy.

McCrone was a prodigious researcher, authoring and coauthoring more than 600 technical articles and 16 books or chapters. He was instrumental in promoting the use of microscopy to chemists. *The Particle Atlas,* his best-known publication, written with other McCrone Associates staff members, appeared as a single volume in 1970 and as a six-volume second edition in 1973. Today it is available on CD-ROM and is still recognized as one of the best handbooks available for solving materials analysis problems. For 30 years, McCrone edited and published *The Microscope,* an international quarterly journal of microscopy that was started by Arthur Barron in 1937 and is dedicated to the advancement of all forms of microscopy for the biologist, mineralogist, metallographer, forensic scientist, and chemist. *The Microscope* publishes original works from the microscopical community and serves as the proceedings of the Inter/Micro microscopy symposium held annually in Chicago.

McCrone's most famous analytical work was his participation in the Shroud of Turin Research Project (STURP). The Shroud of Turin is a length of linen cloth purported to be the burial shroud of Jesus. In 1977, a team of scientists selected by the Holy Shroud Guild—proponents of the shroud's authenticity—proposed a series of tests to determine the shroud's origins. The archbishop of Turin granted permission, and the STURP scientists conducted their testing over five days in 1978. McCrone, upon analyzing the samples he had, concluded that the red stains that had been pointed to as blood were actually pigment—specifically, red ochre and vermilion tempera paint. Two others on the STURP team published their own peer-reviewed analysis, which concluded that the stains were blood. Neither team member was a forensic serologist or a pigment expert. Later presentations at scientific meetings explained how results similar to theirs could be obtained from tempera paint. McCrone adhered to his opinion that comparison of microscopic images showed that the stain on the shroud was not blood.

McCrone resigned from the STURP team in June 1980. Until his death in 2002, he continued to comment on and explain the analysis he had performed, and he became a prominent figure in the ongoing Shroud of Turin controversy. *Judgment Day for the Shroud of Turin,* his book on the subject, was published in 1999. McCrone's contentious conclusion that the Turin shroud is a medieval painting was subsequently vindicated by carbon-14 dating in 1988. In 2000, he received the American Chemical Society National Award in analytical chemistry for his work on the Turin shroud and for his tireless patience in the defense of his work for nearly 20 years.

further from the truth. Microscopy requires the student (and the expert) to know a great deal about many things, how they are made, how they are used, and their physical and chemical natures. This section explains the minimum necessary to understand the microscopic analysis of hairs and fibers. (A complete explanation of microscopy and the optical principles involved is beyond the scope of this book. Additional books and other reference works on this topic, however, can be found in the Further Reading section.)

Microscopy can be applied to nearly every area of the forensic sciences, not just trace evidence. Nowadays, the first reaction for many scientists would be to process a sample for instrumental analysis, using a spectrometer or a chromatograph. They do not realize that much more information can be gleaned from a specimen by viewing it microscopically. Microscopy, additionally, can be quick, inexpensive, simple, and nondestructive. Some of the areas of forensic science investigation where microscopy can play a role are listed in the following table.

A SELECTION OF AREAS OF FORENSIC SCIENCE INVESTIGATION WHERE MICROSCOPY PLAYS A ROLE

art forgeries	minerals
asbestos	paint
building materials	paper
bullets	photographic analysis
chemistry	pollen
drugs	polymers
dust	product tampering
fibers	questioned documents
fingerprints	serology
food poisoning	soil
glass	tapes
hairs	toolmarks
handwriting	wood

A thorough understanding of microscopy therefore is a key component of becoming a good and responsible forensic scientist.

MAGNIFICATION SYSTEMS

Look around—there may be a lens in a nearby area. Eyeglasses, a reading magnifier, and the like are common instruments in daily life. A lens to be used in microscopy, on the other hand, is a very specific instrument. A lens is a translucent material that bends light in a known and predictable manner. For example, an ideal converging lens causes all light entering the lens from one side of the lens to meet again (causing it to converge, or come together) at a point on the other side of the lens. An

The 10× magnification of a human fingertip, showing ridges in the fingerprint and sweat glands *(Cloud Hills Imaging, Ltd., Corbis)*

Friction ridge figure on a finger under a lens *(Shutterstock)*

ideal diverging lens (the other major type of simple lens) causes all light entering from one side to radiate out through the other side as if from a single point of light. In either case, the lens produces an image of the original object but at a different size than the original.

Using geometry, the size and position of an image produced by a lens can be determined; this is based on the focal length of the lens. The focal length is the distance between the two points of focus on either side of the lens, typically the eye and the object being viewed. Much of the image quality in microscopy is determined by focal length and the quality of the lenses. When a person's eyes are too far from or too close to an object, the object cannot be clearly seen because human eyes, being curved, cannot maintain a clear point of focus for all distances. At about 10 inches (25 cm), a human eye can easily distinguish between two objects next to each other; this is the focal length for most people. Lenses are crafted using this "ideal" viewing distance, or focal length.

The minimum distance that two objects can be separated and still be seen as two objects is called its resolution. At a distance of 10 inches (25 cm) from an object, the resolution of the human eye is between 0.15 and 0.30 mm. To distinguish between smaller or closer objects— for instance, to distinguish smaller distances between the markings on

Focal Length

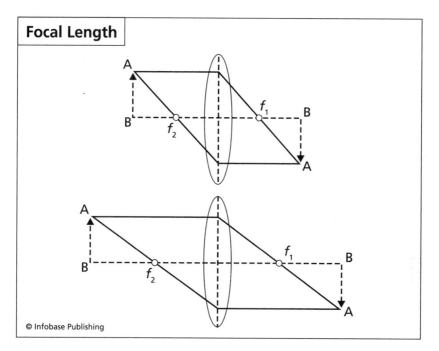

© Infobase Publishing

Focal length, the distance between the two points of focus on either side of a lens, is important in microscopy because it determines much of the image quality.

a postage stamp—some type of assistance is needed. The image must be clearly enlarged or magnified.

A hand lens magnifies an image. Its magnifying strength is indicated by the factor by which it magnifies an image. For example, a lens that enlarges an image to four times its original size is called a "4×" lens, pronounced "four ex" or "four times." Beyond a certain point, however, magnification with one lens cannot continue. In order to bend the light more and make a larger image, as magnification increases, lens diameter decreases. A simple lens that magnifies 1,000× would be only 0.12 mm in diameter! As a result, about 10× to 15× is the practical limit of magnification for single lenses. To achieve greater magnification, a combination of lenses is needed.

A compound microscope, as the name implies, combines a series of lenses into a magnification system to exceed the limits of single simple lenses. A second lens is placed in line with the first lens, and this further enlarges the image: The powers of the two lenses multiply. The total

magnification of the microscope is the product of the two lenses, literally. For example, a 10× lens and a 4× lens would produce a 40× image
(10 × 4 = 40), or one that has been magnified 40 times. Lenses of up to
40× can be used in a compound microscope.

All lenses, even lens systems, have limits, however. When an image
is magnified but its resolution does not improve, a phenomenon called
empty magnification results. Empty magnification yields a larger but
fuzzier-looking image—that is, it is larger but contains less information
than before.

THE MICROSCOPE

The fundamental design of the microscope has not changed much since
its invention. Every component has been improved, either alone or in
combination, to the point where even the most inexpensive microscopes
are suitable for basic applications. The basic parts of a microscope are
depicted in the accompanying photograph.

From the user's point of view, the first part of the microscope one
sees is the eyepieces. The eyepiece, also called the ocular, is the lens that
a person looks into when viewing an object microscopically. A microscope may have one eyepiece (monocular) or two eyepieces (binocular);
most microscopes found in laboratories today are binocular. Eyepieces
usually have a magnification of 10×; one will be focusable, allowing the
viewer to adjust the eyepieces if one eye is stronger than the other, while
the other will be fixed-focus. The area viewed when looking through
the eyepieces is called the field of view, and this will change when the
specimen is moved or the magnification is changed.

Moving down the microscope, the next lens is called the objective
lens (or just "the objective"), as it is closest to the object or specimen
being examined. Without a doubt, the objective is the most important
part of the microscope. Objectives come in a wide variety of types and
differing magnifications (such as 4×, 10×, 15×, 20×, and 25× or higher).
Every objective has different characteristics and, therefore, will be used
in different situations and for different applications. To make selection
of the objective easier, each objective has information about it engraved
into its body in a specific format, including magnification, numerical
aperture, tube length, and the thickness of the coverslip that should be

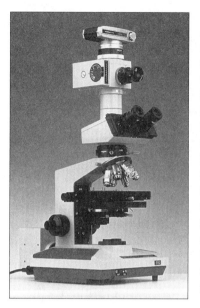

An Olympus optical microscope with a camera attached for photography. The camera (at top center) has a focusing unit and eyepiece immediately below it. Below these are the two eyepieces (binocular) for viewing the specimen. The lens unit of the microscope (at center) contains a selection of lenses that can be rotated for a choice of magnification. Under the lens unit is the specimen table. At bottom center is the light box which supplies light upwards toward the specimen table. Between the light source and the specimen table are different kinds of filters to vary the amount and color of illumination. *(Astrid and Hanns-Frieder Michler/Photo Researchers, Inc.)*

used with the objective; these will all be explained in turn. The magnification has been discussed and will be designated by the power of the lens (10×, 20×, and so on). The numerical aperture is an angular measure of the lens's light-gathering ability and its ability to resolve an image. Remember, better resolution is the key to good microscopy; magnification without resolution results in a large blurry image (empty magnification). The tube length is the distance from the lowest part of the objective to the upper edge of the eyepiece; this has been standardized at 160 millimeters in modern microscopes. Because the tube length determines where the focused image will appear, the objectives must be designed and constructed for a specific tube length. Coverslips, the thin glass plates that are placed on top of mounted specimens, protect the specimen and the objective from damage. They come in a range of thicknesses measured in millimeters (0.17 mm, for example). All of this information is important to the microscopist's proper selection of a particular objective.

Objectives come in a variety of types, each with specific benefits and limitations. Achromatic objectives, or achromats, are the least expensive objectives and they are found on most microscopes. These objectives are designed to be corrected for chromatic aberration, a situation in which white light from the specimen is broken out into multiple colored images at various distances from the lens. Chromatic aberration results from defects in the lens that make it act like a prism, splitting the white light into its component colors. Achromats are corrected for red and blue only, and this can lead to substantial artifacts (distortions), such as colored halos. Because of this, it may be necessary to use a green filter and employ black-and-white film for photomicrography.

A simple lens focuses a flat specimen on a microscope slide onto the lens, which has a rounded surface. This potential distortion, called curvature of field, results in only part of the image being in focus. The middle would be in focus, for example, but the edges would be blurry. Regular objectives, called apochromats, lack correction for flatness of field, but most manufacturers have started to offer flat-field corrections for achromat objectives, called plan achromats.

Another common distortion in a lens, called astigmatism or spherical aberration, results from a lens not adequately spherical. This defect makes specimen images appear to be "pulled" in one direction—circles would appear oblong. The light passing near the center of the lens is less refracted than the light at the edge of the lens, and this distorts the image in that direction. (Refraction, or the bending of light as it passes from one medium into another, will be discussed later in this chapter.) Because this is a major fault and greatly hampers the viewing of samples, most modern microscope objectives are corrected for spherical aberration.

Semi-apochromats, commonly called fluorites because the mineral fluorite was the original material used for correction, represent an improvement over other lenses. Similar to achromats, fluorites correct for chromatic aberration for two colors, but they also correct for spherical aberration in (typically) two colors. Fluorite objectives are now made with advanced glass formulations that contain fluorspar or synthetic substitutes. Fluorites have a higher numerical aperture, better resolution, and higher contrast; fluorite objectives, of course, cost more than achromats.

The most highly corrected objectives are the apochromats, which are almost like mini-lens systems within one objective. Apochromats have several internal lenses with different thicknesses and curvatures; their configuration is unique to apochromats. Apochromats are corrected for three colors—red, green, and blue—and, because of this, they have almost no chromatic aberration. They are among the most expensive lenses, but they provide even better numerical aperture and resolution than fluorites.

As noted earlier in this section, in a typical microscope the tube length (distance from the top of the eyepiece to the bottom of the objective) is set to 160 millimeters. Since the mid-1990s, however, the major microscope manufacturers have migrated to infinity-corrected lens systems. In these systems, the image distance is essentially set to infinity, instead of the standard 160 millimeters, and a lens is placed within the body of the microscope between the objective and the eyepieces to produce an intermediate image. Older finite, or fixed tube length, microscopes have a specified distance from the nosepiece opening, where the objective lens attaches, to the eyepieces. In these older microscopes, this distance is referred to as the mechanical tube length of the microscope. This kind of design assumes that when the microscope is focused on the specimen, the specimen is only a few microns away from the front focal plane of the objective. Finite tube lengths were standardized at 160 millimeters during the 19th century by the Royal Microscopical Society and were the main design for over 100 years. As microscopy become more complex and new examinations could be conducted with the addition of optical accessories, problems arose. The addition of these optical accessories, such as analytical filters or lenses, into the light path of a fixed tube length microscope increased the effective tube length to a value greater than 160 millimeters. This created poor images, as all the lenses were designed for that specific tube length: Adding a vertical reflected light illuminator, polarizing intermediate stage, or similar attachment introduced aberrations into an otherwise perfectly-corrected optical system. Manufacturers were forced to introduce adapters and "fixes" into these accessories to re-establish the effective 160-millimeter tube length of the microscope system. This resulted in increased magnification, loss of resolution, reduced light intensities, and ultimately poorer images.

In a finite optical system of fixed tube length, light passing through the objective is directed toward the intermediate image plane (located at the front focal plane of the eyepiece) and converges at that point, undergoing constructive and destructive interference to produce an image. This is not the situation for infinity-corrected optical systems. The infinity-corrected objective produces a flux of parallel light wave trains imaged at infinity; these are focused at the intermediate image plane by the tube lens. Objectives designed for infinity-corrected microscopes are not interchangeable with those intended for a finite (160 millimeters) optical tube length microscope. Infinity lenses demonstrate spherical aberration when used on a finite microscope system because of a lack of a tube lens.

The objective and tube lens together form a compound objective lens system that produces an intermediate image at a finite distance within the microscope tube. Location of the tube lens with respect to the objective is of primary concern when designing infinity-corrected microscopes. The region between the objective and tube lens (infinity space) provides a path of parallel light rays into which complex optical components can be placed without the introduction of spherical aberration or modification of the objective working distance. In fact, parfocality (the ability of a lens or lens set to have corresponding focal points in the same plane) between different objectives in a matched set can be maintained with infinity-corrected microscopes, even when one or two auxiliary components are added to the optical path. Another major benefit is that accessories can be designed to produce an exact 1× magnification value without altering the alignment between the objective and tube lens. This feature allows comparison of specimens using a combination of several optical techniques. This is possible because optical accessories placed into a set of parallel light waves do not shift the location (either laterally or axially) nor the focal point of the image.

Longer objective focal lengths utilized in infinity optical systems require correspondingly larger working distances to match. Increasing the parfocal distance of the objective is almost the same as achieving a significant increase in working distance, particularly for lower magnification objectives. With a 1× objective, as an example, the calculation for magnification for infinity-corrected systems states that objective and tube lens focal lengths should be the same. Therefore, in a system with a 200-millimeter tube lens focal length, a longer parfocal distance is required to use an objective with such a low magnification. Formulae show that magnifications as low as 0.5× can be obtained with 200-millimeter tube lens focal lengths. Practically speaking, the shorter focal lengths restrict the minimum objective magnification to just above the 1× range.

In microscopy, numerical aperture is the single most important feature of a lens. This is because of the lens' ability to bend light and the nature of light itself. Numerical aperture is an angular measure of the light-gathering ability and the resolving quality of a lens. As discussed earlier, a certain minimum distance between two points in a specimen is necessary to allow them to be seen as separate. This distance (d) varies depending on the numerical aperture (NA), as can be seen in the following equation:

$$d = \lambda/2NA$$

In prose, the equation states that the minimum distance that preserves a visible distinction between two points is the quotient of the wavelength of light (λ) and twice the numerical aperture of the lens. The numerical aperture itself is mathematically defined as follows:

$$NA = n \sin u$$

where n is the refractive index of the medium between the coverslip and the front lens (usually air), and u is half the angle of aperture of the objective. Refractive index is discussed further in the next section, but briefly, the refractive index of a medium is the ratio of the speed of light (for a given wavelength) in a vacuum to its speed in the medium. The refractive index of air is 1.0003; practically speaking, this means the NA of any lens system with air as the intermediate medium will be less than 1 because half of the angle u in air cannot be more than 90 degrees. Put another way, all materials—samples, lenses, or mounting media—will bend light more than air will.

The resolving power of the human eye or the objective lens is not sufficient for a magnification of, for example, 10,000×, because two points can only be seen as separate if the distance between them is within the limit of the resolving power. If the distance is below the resolving power, separation between the two objects would not be visible; if it is higher, one could see only two (and not several) points with no more detail than before. The maximum magnification available, therefore, is about 1,000 times the NA of the objective.

The microscope stage is a geared platform upon which the specimen sits during viewing. The stage is moveable right and left, forward and backward to position the specimen; it can also be moved up or down

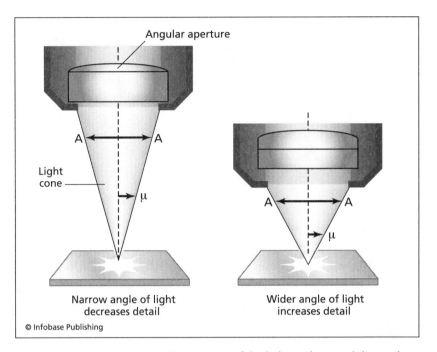

Numerical aperture is an angular measure of the light-gathering ability and, ultimately, of the resolving quality of a lens (its ability to distinguish between two close but separate points).

to focus the specimen image, meaning that portion of the specimen in the field of view is sitting in the same horizontal plane. Stages are equipped with a coarse (large movement) and a fine (minute movement) focus. Stages may be mechanical (that is, having knobs for control of movement), rotating (able to spin in 360 degrees but not move back and forth), or both.

The condenser lens is used to obtain a bright, even field of illumination and improve image resolution. Condensers are lenses below the stage that focus (condense) light onto the specimen field of view. Condensers also have their own condenser diaphragm, which controls the amount of light focused and adjusts for contrast in the image. The condenser diaphragm is different from the field diaphragm, a control that allows more or less light into the entire lens system of the microscope. An inexperienced microscopist may use the condenser diaphragm to adjust the brightness in the field of view; this is a mistake. The condenser diaphragm

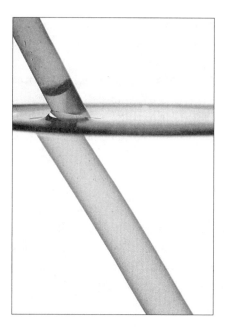

The refractive index of air (1.0003) is very different from that of water, meaning that a light ray bends more passing through water than air, as evidenced by the photograph of the drinking straw refracted by water. *(www.shutterstock.com)*

controls contrast and the image quality will suffer greatly if it is used to adjust brightness; the field diaphragm should be used for brightness.

The illumination of the microscope is more complicated than turning on a lightbulb. Illumination is a key component in a quality microscopic image. There are two main types of illumination in microscopy—critical and Köhler. Critical illumination concentrates the light on the specimen using the condenser lens. Critical illumination produces an intense, but uneven, lighting that highlights edges. Köhler illumination, named after German microscopist August Köhler, aligns the light rays parallel to each other throughout the lens system; this evenly illuminates the specimen. Introduced in 1893, Köhler illumination is considered the standard configuration for microscopic illumination.

REFRACTIVE INDEX

The refraction of visible light is an important characteristic of lenses that allows them to focus a beam of light onto a single point. Refraction (or the bending of light) occurs as light passes from a one medium to another when there is a difference in the index of refraction between the two materials. It is responsible for a variety of familiar phenomena such as the apparent distortion of objects partially submerged in water. The refraction of light is also a phenomenon used in the analysis of trace evidence, particularly fibers.

Refractive index is defined as the relative speed at which light moves through a material with respect to its speed in a vacuum. By convention, the refractive index of a vacuum is defined as having a value of 1.0. The index of refraction, N (or n), of other transparent materials is defined through the equation

$$N = C/v$$

where C is the speed of light and v is the velocity of light in that material. Because the refractive index of a vacuum is defined as 1.0 and a vacuum is devoid of any material, the refractive indices of all transparent materials are greater than 1.0. For most practical purposes, the refractive index of light through air (1.0003) can be used to calculate refractive indices of unknown materials. Refractive indices of some common materials are presented in the following table.

When light passes from a less dense medium (such as air) to a denser medium (such as water), the speed of the light wave decreases. Alternatively, when light passes from a denser medium (water) to a less dense medium (air), the speed of the wave increases. The angle of refracted light is dependent upon both the composition of the material through which it passes and the angle of incidence (the angle at which light strikes the material). The angle of incidence is measured against the

THE REFRACTIVE INDICES OF SEVERAL KNOWN MATERIALS

Material	Refractive Index (RI)
air	1.0003
ice	1.310
water	1.330
glass, soda lime	1.510
ruby	1.760
diamond	2.417

normal, defined as a line perpendicular to the boundary between two substances. The light passes into the boundary at an angle to the surface and will be refracted according to Snell's Law:

$$N_1 \times \sin(q_1) = N_2 \times \sin(q_2)$$

where N represents the refractive indices of material 1 and material 2, and q represents the angles of light traveling through these materials with respect to the normal. When N_1 is greater than N_2, the angle of refraction is always smaller than the angle of incidence. However, when N_2 is greater than N_1, the angle of refraction is always greater than the angle of incidence. When the two refractive indices are equal ($N_1 = N_2$), then the light passes through without refraction. Either of the first two conditions are useful for determining if the refractive index of a sample is higher or lower than the mounting medium it is in. The third condition, equality of refractive indices, allows a microscopist to determine the exact refractive index of a sample. The sample is placed in a series of liquids of known refractive value and when the sample disappears, it means the refractive index of the sample and the liquid are the same. Samples to be viewed in transmitted light must be mounted in a material with a refractive index that is close that of the sample. If the refractive indices are too different, the images will have excessive contrast and be blurred. The refractive index of water is about 1.33 and the refractive index of hair is about 1.5, which means that water makes a poor mounting medium, or mountant, because it refracts the light so much less than a hair. Many materials are commercially available to use as mountants, and their refractive indices are around 1.5.

Named after Friedrich Johann Karl Becke (1855–1931), a noted Austrian geologist, mineralogist, and petrologist, a Becke line is a band or rim of light visible along an object's boundary in plane-polarized light. Materials tend to be thicker in the middle and thinner towards the edges; they act as lenses because of their shape. If the refractive index is higher than the surrounding mounting medium, the rays move toward the center of the material; if the refractive index is lower than the surrounding mounting medium, the light rays diverge toward the edge of the material. The scientist, knowing the refractive index of the mounting medium, can now estimate if the sample has a higher or lower refractive index than the mounting medium. Oils of known refractive index (to 4 decimal places) are sold for this method.

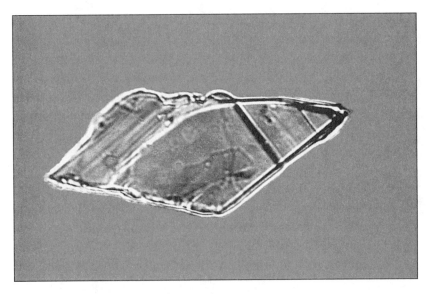

The Becke line *(Photo Researchers, Inc.)*

POLARIZED LIGHT MICROSCOPY

As useful as a microscope is, it truly comes into its own as an analytical instrument when it is outfitted with a series of filters. These filters change a microscope into a polarizing light microscope (PLM), a tool of nearly infinite applications. The PLM uses optical properties of materials to reveal their internal structure and composition. This information leads to the identification and characterization of samples.

To know how a PLM works, it is necessary to know how ordinary light works. Ordinary, unfiltered light emanates from a source, such as a bulb, in all directions. With light acting like a wave, all directions of vibration are equally possible. If the light passes through a special filter, called a polarizer, the resulting filtered light vibrates only in one, preferred direction. Polarized light is not "visible" to viewers, but most people have seen polarized light through polarized sunglasses. The polarized lenses of the sunglasses reduce glare, like from a car hood on a sunny day, by filtering out all the light except for that traveling in the direction preferred by the lens. The filter absorbs all the light traveling in the "wrong" direction. The PLM exploits this phenomenon by causing light rays to interact with sample materials in particular ways.

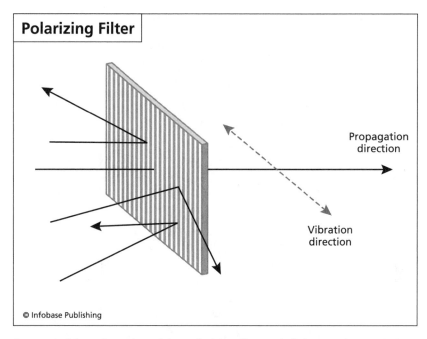

Polarizing Filter

Propagation direction

Vibration direction

© Infobase Publishing

Because of the orientation of the polarizing filter, only light rays that are in line with its orientation can pass through. This is how polarized sunglasses work, by filtering out scattered light rays and only allowing certain ones through.

Materials fall into one of two categories—isotropic or anisotropic materials. Isotropic materials are those that demonstrate the same optical properties in all directions, such as gases, liquids, and certain glasses. Because they are optically the same in all directions, isotropic materials have only one refractive index. Light, therefore, passes through them at the same speed, with no changes in speed.

Anisotropic materials, on the other hand, have optical properties that vary with the orientation of the incoming light and the optical structure of the material; around 90 percent of all solid materials fall into this category. The RIs of anisotropic materials vary depending on both the direction of the incident light and the material's optical structure. Anisotropic materials can be thought of as having a "grain," like wood, with an internal orientation.

To manipulate the light interacting with a sample, a PLM uses two polarizing filters (or polarizers, sometimes called polars, for short),

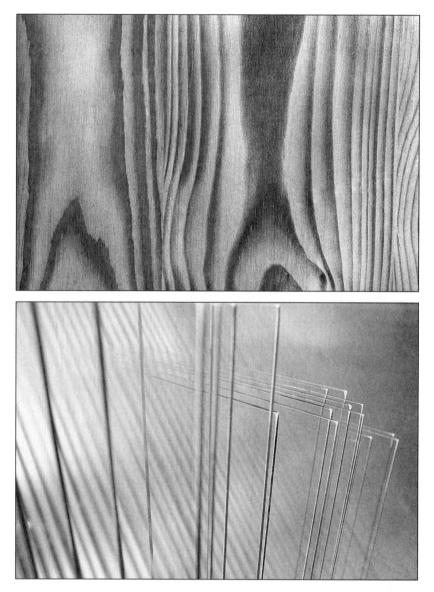

Isotropic materials have the same optical properties in all directions, whereas anisotropic ones have differing properties based on the incident light and the internal structure of the material. Anisotropic materials can be envisioned as having a "grain." A close-up photograph of natural wood (anisotropic) and a photograph of tempered toughened glass (isotropic) in a storage rack illustrate these properties. *(www.shutterstock.com and © Huw Jones/Alamy)*

called the polarizer and the analyzer. The polarizer sits beneath the stage, and its preferred vibration direction is right-to-left (sometimes called the "east-west" direction, like on a map). The analyzer, which prefers light that vibrates perpendicular to the polarizer (that is, in the "north-south" direction), is located above the objective.

The microscopist can slide the analyzer into or out of the light path; the polarizer is fixed below the condenser. Both filters can be rotated and the dials are marked for setting the angles accurately. As the two filters come into alignment, more of the available light is screened out by either the polarizer (setting the first obstacle of a preferred direction) or the analyzer (as light that comes through the polarizer meets some of the requirements of the analyzer). When the preferred pathways of the two filters are at right angles to each other, the field of view appears black or very, very dark. Why is this? In this configuration, no light can meet the requirements of the two filters—they have directly competing orientations. At this point, the filters are said to be crossed, and no light can pass through the microscope to the viewer's eyes. Surprisingly, this is a useful feature of the PLM: The scientist can obtain information both in plane-polarized light (with only the polarizer in place) or with crossed polarizers (both polarizer and analyzer in place). But if no light is coming through, how can that be useful?

The material under analysis, of course, refracts the filtered light in its characteristic way. Viewed in plane-polarized light, transparent or translucent materials appear much as they do when viewed in natural light—that is, until the specimen is rotated on the stage (on the optical axis of the microscope). As the specimen moves through the preferred orientation of the polarizer, its brightness or color may appear to change. This apparent variation of color is called pleochroism. Only anisotropic materials display pleochroism: The internal "grain" of the material causes the light to leave the material at varying angles. When this refracted light encounters the oriented polarized filter, it is more or less blocked, and the human eye perceives this as a change in the color of the anisotropic material.

Anisotropic materials have at least two refractive indices because of their internal organization. Light passing through them is split into two rays, creating two pathways for the light rays, one faster and one slower.

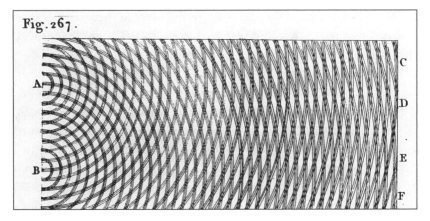

Drawing of two-source interference patterns from the book *A Course of Lectures on Natural Philosophy and the Mechanical Arts* by Thomas A. Young *(AIP Emilio Segrè Visual Archives, Brittle Books Collection)*

The speed is dependent on the amount or "optical density" of the internal organization: Like a highway, it is faster to travel with traffic than across it. In the same way, light passing along the more organized axis (with traffic) moves faster because the material allows it, whereas the the light passing along the less organized axis (across traffic) moves more slowly. Therefore, the faster light ray comes out of the sample before the slower light ray. When an anisotropic material is placed under crossed polarizers (at right angles to each other) and rotated on the optical axis of the microscope, colors called interference colors result. These colors are caused by the destructive interference of the anisotropic material's two light rays; that is, the two light rays cancel each other out more or less. Since the two light rays travel through the specimen at different speeds (one faster than the other), each has its own RI. The numerical difference between the RI of the fast light ray and the RI of slow light ray is called birefringence. Only the components of the two light rays traveling in the same direction in the same plane will recombine at the analyzer. At this point, they can interfere with each other constructively and destructively, canceling each other out to a greater or lesser degree, resulting in the interference colors. The colors are not a spectrum: they are a series of colors referred to as Newton's series; they are the same colors seen on a soap bubble or an oil slick.

Different materials have different optical properties, like refractive index and birefringence. Using a PLM, a scientist can learn a little or a lot about almost every kind of material, from asbestos to zircon. Few scientists routinely use a PLM, however, probably because they have not learned how to use it properly or in routine work.

FLUORESCENCE MICROSCOPY

Besides conventional microscopy and the PLM, another method of microscopy that is useful in the analysis of forensic trace evidence is fluorescence microscopy. Like the PLM, a fluorescence microscope uses filters to select specific types of light that, when they interact with the sample, provide information. Fluorescence (as well as phosphorescence) is the luminescence of a substance excited by radiation. Phosphorescence is characterized by long-lived emission, like the luminous numbers and hands on a "glow-in-the-dark" watch face. Fluorescence, by contrast, is shorter lived; for instance, a white T-shirt glows in the presence of a black light but stops glowing when the light is turned off.

Luminescence occurs when radiation of high energy falls on a substance and excites it, infusing it with energy. The substance absorbs or converts a certain, small part of the energy (into heat, for example). Most of the energy that is not absorbed by the substance is emitted again. In fluorescence, the wavelength of the emitted energy is longer than that of the exciting radiation because the radiation has lost energy compared to the exciting radiation. Therefore, invisible radiation can cause a fluorescing substance to emit energy in the visible range, creating a colored glow. This is the basis of fluorescence microscopy.

In a fluorescence microscope, the specimen is illuminated with light of a short wavelength—for example, ultraviolet or blue; the specimen absorbs part of this light and reemits it as fluorescence. The wavelength of light is selected using a filter to channel only light of a specific wavelength; this is called the excitation filter. The fluorescence emitted is relatively weak compared with the strong illumination that caused it. To see the fluorescence, the light used to excite the sample is filtered out by a secondary filter placed between the specimen and the eye; this filter is called, for obvious reasons, a barrier filter. This filter, in principle, should be fully opaque at the wavelength used for excitation and fully transparent at longer wavelengths so as to transmit the fluorescence. The fluorescent object is therefore seen as a bright image against a dark background. A fluorescence microscope differs from a conventional microscope in that it has a special light source and a pair of complementary filters. The lamp is a powerful light source, rich in short wavelengths: high-pressure mercury arc lamps are the most common.

Fluorescence microscopy assists with discriminating between samples with similar but not the same characteristics, particularly dyes or colorants. Some materials respond differently based on the fluorescent chemicals in them—the differences are seen as various colors and intensities.

Microscopy is a powerful technique for forensic scientists to use on the smallest possible evidence traces. It does require an understanding of optics and lenses, but the basics are not difficult to master. With an inexpensive microscope and a few chemicals, one can perform an amazing array of analytical tests and examinations.

With microscopes to identify evidence and its morphology and the spectrometers to analyze its chemistry, there is little that cannot be made sense of in a forensic laboratory.

3

Hairs

One of the most frequently recovered types of evidence is also one of the most misunderstood: hairs. Hairs make good forensic evidence because they are sturdy and can survive for many years, they carry a lot of biological information, and they are easy and cost-effective to examine. DNA can also be extracted from hairs, and this adds to their forensic utility.

Although a few cases of poor forensic hair examination have gathered media attention, especially in cases where samples have been reexamined after someone has been convicted, the fault often lies more with the examiner than with the method. Hairs can offer strong investigative and courtroom information, but only when examined properly, reported on conservatively, and testified about accurately.

GROWTH OF HAIRS

Hairs are a particular structure common only to mammals—they are the fibrous growths that originate from the skin of that class of animal. Other animals have structures that may appear to be hairs or may even

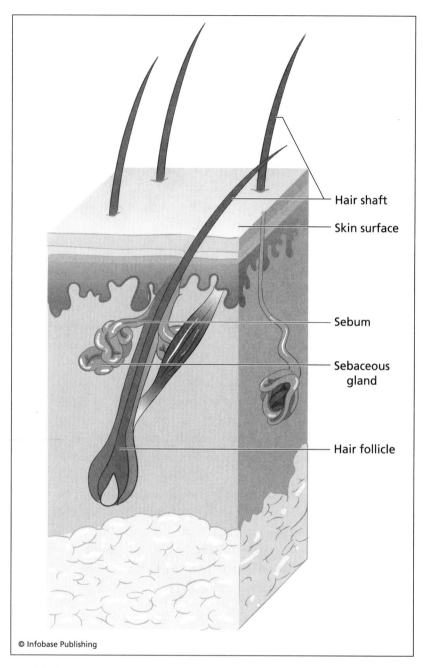

Hair shaft

Skin surface

Sebum

Sebaceous gland

Hair follicle

© Infobase Publishing

The follicle is the structure within which hairs grow; it is a roughly cylindrical tube with a larger pit at the bottom. Hairs grow from the base of the follicle upwards.

be called hairs, but they are not: Only mammals have hairs. Humans use hairs as signs of culture, status, and gender, as well as for personal or artistic expression.

Hairs grow from the skin, or, more precisely, the epidermis, of the body. The follicle is the structure within which hairs grow; it is a roughly cylindrical tube with a larger pit at the bottom. Hairs grow from the base of the follicle upwards. In the base of the follicle, the hair is still very soft; as the hair proceeds up the follicle, it slowly begins to harden and dry out. Hair is made of keratin, a tough, protein-based material that makes hair, nails, and horns in animals. The hardening process of hair growth is therefore called keratinization. Hair is one of the most durable materials produced by nature and hairs from mummies, both natural and cultural in origin, have been found thousands of years after the person's death. Keratinization also explains why it does not hurt when a person's hair is cut: Hair is "dead" from the moment it peeks above the skin. The only place hair is "alive" is in the base of the follicle, which is why it *does* hurt when a hair gets pulled out.

The follicle contains other structures, such as blood vessels, nerves, and sebaceous glands, the last producing oils that coat our hairs, helping

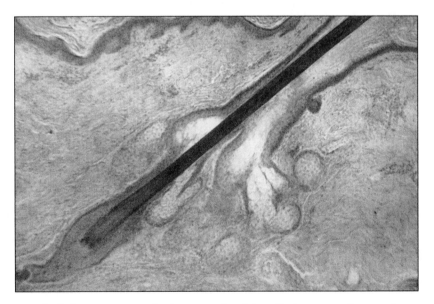

Hair shaft showing root and sebaceous gland that discharge an oily secretion into hair follicles *(Lester V. Bergman/CORBIS)*

to keep them soft and pliable. Hairs even have muscles, called pili arrector muscles (*pilus* is the Latin word for "hair"), which raise hairs when a person gets chilled (so-called goose bumps).

Hairs go through three phases of growth. In the anagen, or actively growing, phase, the follicle is producing new cells and pushing them up the hair shaft as they become incorporated into the structure of the hair. The hair is moved up the shaft by a mechanical method. As the cells are produced, the opposing scales of the hair and the follicle "ratchet" the hair up the shaft—much like gears in a machine! Between this mechanical method and the upward pressure from the growth of the cells in the follicle, the hairs grow outward from the skin.

Specialized cells in the follicle produce small colored granules, called melanin or pigment, that give hairs their particular color; these cells are called melanocytes. Only two types of melanin are found in hairs: a dark brown pigment called eumelanin and a lighter pigment called phaeomelanin. The combination, density, and distribution of these granules produce the range of hair colors seen in humans and animals.

After the active growth phase, the hair transitions into a resting phase; this transitional phase is called the catagen phase. During catagen phase, the follicle begins to shut down production of cells; the cells begin to shrink; and the root condenses into a bulb-shaped structure called, understandably, a bulb root or a club root.

The telogen phase is the resting phase for the follicle—cell production has ceased completely, and the root has condensed into a bulb held in place only by a mechanical connection at the base of the root/follicle. When this mechanical connection breaks (through combing, brushing, or normal wear), the follicle is triggered into anagen phase again and the cycle renews. On a healthy human head of hair, about 80 to 90 percent of the hairs are in anagen phase, about 2 percent in catagen phase, and about 10 to 18 percent in telogen phase. When the telogen hairs are removed, new hairs begin to grow at once; clipping and shaving have no effect on growth. The time required for human follicles to regrow hairs varies from 147 days for scalp hairs to 61 days for eyebrow hairs. Humans, on average, lose about 100 scalp hairs a day; this provides for an adequate and constant source of potential evidence for transfer and collection.

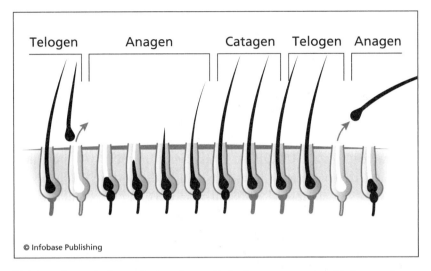

Telogen   Anagen   Catagen   Telogen   Anagen

© Infobase Publishing

Hairs go through three phases of growth. In the anagen, or actively growing, phase, the follicle is producing new cells and pushing them up the hair shaft as they become incorporated into the structure of the hair. After the active growth phase, the hair transitions into a resting phase; this transitional phase is called the catagen phase. During catagen phase, the follicle begins to shut down production of cells. Telogen phase is the resting phase for the follicle—cell production has ceased completely, and the root has condensed into a bulb held in place only by a mechanical connection at the base of the root/follicle. When this mechanical connection breaks (through combing, brushing, or normal wear), the follicle is triggered into anagen phase again and the cycle renews.

Forensic hair examiners are sometimes asked if they can determine if a hair was removed forcibly, during a struggle or assault, for example, to document the severity of the assault. This is a difficult question. If the hair has a bulb root (meaning it was removed during telogen phase), then obviously the question cannot be answered. If tissue from the follicle is attached to the root, then the hair was removed during anagen or possibly catagen phase, that is, while the hair and the follicle were attached through active cellular growth. Because the actively growing hair is still soft and unkeratinized, the root may have stretched before being torn out of the follicle. Therefore, if the root is stretched *and* has follicular tissue attached, the examiner may state that the hair was forcibly removed. That does not, however, tell the examiner what *kind* of force was used—a violent assault, hair being caught in something, or a friendly wrestling match—and the examiner must be cautious about making unsupportable statements.

MICROANATOMY

A hair is a complicated composite material with many intricately organized structures, only some of which are visible under the microscope. On the macro scale (that is, visible without magnification), a single hair has a root, a shaft, and a tip. The root is the portion that formerly was in the follicle. The shaft is the main portion of the hair. The tip is the portion of the hair that is farthest from the body. In discussing parts of a hair, forensic scientists describe directions as proximal, meaning toward the body, or distal, meaning away from the body; the root is the most proximal part of the hair, while the tip is the most distal.

Internally, hairs have a variable and complex microanatomy. The three main structural elements in a hair are the cuticle, the cortex, and the medulla. The cuticle of a hair is a series of overlapping layers of scales that form a protective covering. Animal hairs have scale patterns that vary by species, and these patterns are a useful diagnostic tool for identifying animal hairs. Humans have a scale pattern called imbricate, but it is fairly common among animals and, despite attempts to use scales as an individualizing tool for human hairs, is not generally useful in forensic examinations.

The next structure is the cortex, which makes up the bulk of the hair. The cortex consists of spindle-shaped cells (sometimes called fusiform) that contain or constrain numerous other structures. Pigment granules are found in the cortex and are dispersed variably throughout the cortex. The granules vary in size, shape, aggregation, and distribution—all excellent characteristics for forensic comparisons. Small bubbles, called cortical fusi, may appear in the cortex; when they do appear, they may be sparse, aggregated, or evenly distributed throughout the cortex. Cortical fusi also vary in size and shape. Many telogen root hairs will have an aggregate of cortical fusi near the root bulb; it is thought that this is related to the shut down of the growth activity as the follicle transitions from catagen to telogen phase.

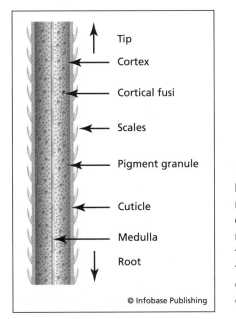

Tip
Cortex
Cortical fusi
Scales
Pigment granule
Cuticle
Medulla
Root

© Infobase Publishing

Hairs are composed of three main parts: The cuticle, layers of overlapping scales, the cortex, the main mass of the hair cells where the pigmentation resides, and the medulla, a series of variably expressed hair cells along the central axis of the hair.

Odd structures that look like very large pigment granules, called ovoid bodies, may appear irregularly in the cortex. They may, in fact, *be* large, aggregated, or aberrant pigment granules, but no one knows—little if any research has been conducted on what ovoid bodies are.

HUMAN VERSUS NONHUMAN

It is relatively easy to determine if a hair is human or nonhuman by a simple microscopic examination. (The terms *human* and *nonhuman* are often used instead of "animal" because, technically, humans are also animals.) Determining what kind of nonhuman hair it is, however, may be tricky in some circumstances as, certain animals' hairs can be similar. Animal hairs have several macroscopic characteristics that distinguish their hairs from those of humans.

First of all, animals have three types of hairs. Guard hairs are large stiff hairs that make up the outer part of the animal's coat. Guard hairs are the hairs that should be used for microscopic identification. Guard hairs may have a widening in the upper half of the shaft, called a shield. Below the shield, if it is present, may often be found a sub-shield stricture, a narrowing of the hair to slightly less than the normal, non-shield shaft diameter. A sub-shield stricture may be accompanied by a bend in the shaft at the stricture.

Thinner, softer fur hairs fill in the rest of the coat, providing warmth and bulk. Fur hairs are generic in their appearance and are typically useless for microscopic identification. The root may give an indication as to taxonomic origin, but it may also be misleading; it is best not to use fur hairs for microscopic evaluations.

Finally, animals have vibrissa, the technical term for whiskers—the short to long, stiff, often white hairs around the snout and muzzle. No comprehensive study has been made on the identification of taxonomic origin by vibrissa, probably because these hairs have a long life cycle and are lost comparatively less often than the myriad guard and fur hairs of a typical animal.

Some nonhuman hairs are color banded, showing abrupt color transitions along the shaft of the hair, including the tip. Raccoons, for example, have four color bands in their guard hairs; they are the only animals known to have this many bands in their guard hair.

As noted earlier, scale patterns also may be useful in identifying animal hairs. The best ways to visualize scale patterns are with a scanning electron microscope or by making a scale cast and viewing it with a light microscope. The simplest method of making a scale cast is to brush clear nail polish onto a glass microscope slide and lay the hair in the still-wet polish. Before the polish dries completely, the hair should be gently "peeled" from the polish; a cast of the exterior of the hair remains in the polish. This cast can then be examined on a light microscope.

BODY AREA DETERMINATION

Unlike other animals, humans exhibit a wide variety of hairs on their bodies. The characteristics of these hairs may allow for an estimation of body area origin. The typical body areas that can be determined are head (or scalp), pubic, facial, chest, axillary (armpits), eyelash/eyebrow, and limb. Hairs that do not fit into these categories may be called transitional body hairs, such as those on the stomach, between the chest and the pubic region. The following table lists the characteristics generally associated with the different body hair types.

GENERAL DESCRIPTIONS OF HUMAN BODY-AREA HAIR TRAITS

Type of Body Hair	Diameter	Shaft	Tip
head	even	straight or curly; some waviness; may be very long	usually cut
pubic	varies	buckling*; sometimes extreme waviness or curl	usually pointed; may be razor cut
facial	wide; even	triangular in cross-section; some shouldering**	usually cut; may be scissors or razor cut
chest	even to curly	wavy to curly; some more straight	usually pointed
axillary	even; some variation	less wavy/curly than chest	usually pointed; may be colorless
limb	fine; tapering	slight arc	usually pointed
eyebrow/ eyelash	tapering	arc; short	pointed

Note: * Buckling is an abrupt change in direction of the hair shaft with or without a slight twist, whereas ** shouldering is an asymmetrical cross section of hairs.

In some instances, it may be difficult or impossible for the forensic scientist to make a clear determination as to whether a hair is chest-area or axillary in origin; it may also not matter in regard to the actual circumstances of the crime. Labeling the hair as a "body hair" is sufficient and may be the most accurate conclusion given the quality and nature of the hair.

The determination of what type of body hair a hair in evidence is may have important consequences for a case: In a case involving the identification of an adult pubic-area hair on a preadolescent victim, the hair was important evidence of the circumstances surrounding her death. A girl of that age could not have produced a pubic-area hair—those hairs are generated by the hormones associated with puberty. DNA from the hair was the same as that from the suspect; this, in addition to overwhelming trace evidence associating the suspect with the crime, led to a guilty plea.

ANCESTRAL ESTIMATION

The morphology and color of a hair lying on a surface can give an indication of a person's ancestry. Humans are more variable from one to another in their hair morphology than any other primate. This variation tends to correlate with a person's ancestry (as shown in the table) although it is not an exact correlation. For simplicity and accuracy, three main ancestral groups are used: Europeans, Africans, and Asians. In the older anthropological and forensic literature, these groups were referred to as, respectively, Caucasoids, Negroids, and Mongoloids; these terms are now archaic. They are no better at describing the intended populations than the geographic terms previously listed—Caucasoid/European hair descriptions include some Hispanics and peoples of the Middle East, for example. The geographic terms are as accurate and less offensive.

Typically head and pubic hairs provide the clearest evidence for ancestral estimates. It may be possible with certain other hairs, especially facial hairs, but body hairs should be viewed cautiously. Asians, for example, have less body hair than other populations and,

VARIOUS CHARACTERISTICS OF HAIR BY ANCESTRY

Ancestry	Diameter	Cross Section	Pigment Distribution	Cuticle	Undulation
African	60–90μm	flat	dense; clumped	thin	prevalent
European	70–100μm	oval	even	medium	uncommon
Asian	90–120μm	round	dense to very dense	thick	never

in some areas, may have none. It is important to remember also that these estimates may not line up with how people racially identify themselves.

DAMAGE, DISEASE, AND TREATMENTS

Humans do many different things to their hair, depending on their culture: cutting, dyeing, braiding, even shaving—and these treatments are not limited to just the scalp! In addition, some diseases affect the hairs or the follicles; these are rare but distinctive.

The tips of hairs can provide good information about how the hair has been treated. Scissor-cut hair has a clean, straight border, while razor-cut hair is angled. Flying glass (produced, for instance, in a hit-and-run incident or an explosion) cuts hair in a unique way, leaving a long curved "tail." Burnt hair is blackened and may appear bubbled or expanded. Crushed hair is also easy to recognize.

Bleaching of the hair oxidizes the pigmentation and removes its color. The artificial treatment may stop at this point or a new color may be added to the hair. Coloring hair is much like dyeing wool fibers (both are hair) or other textile fibers. As the hair continues to grow, the point where the bleaching/coloration was applied is visible as an abrupt color change. (The roots show the natural color.) If the length of the natural hair color portion is measured, the examiner can estimate the time interval between the cosmetic treatment and the time the hair was lost. Head hairs grow an average of 0.5 inches (1.3 cm) per month, so the natural portion length in inches is divided by half to yield the approximate number of months.

The diseases that affect hair morphology (shape) are rare, but such hair samplings make them excellent evidence for identifying a source. Pili annulati refers to hairs with colored rings. In pili annulati the hairs have alternating light and dark bands along their length, like tiger or zebra stripes. People with dark hair may have pili annulati but not know it because their hair color masks the condition. Monilethrix makes hairs look like a string of beads (the name comes from the Greek words for "bead" and "hair"). Along the length of the hair are nodes and constrictions making the hair vary in diameter. This hair "beading" weakens the hair, and people suffering from monilethrix have patchy hair loss.

Pili torti is a twisting of the hair along its length, creating a spiral-like morphology. There may be several twists in one hair. The cuticle is present, but the twisting creates stress that leads to fractures in the cuticle and cortex.

Finally, the presence of vermin (such as lice), dandruff, or fungus should also be noted. These traits add to the classification of the hairs, because the hairs come from individuals with these traits.

COMPARISON OF HUMAN HAIRS

The goal of most forensic hair examinations is the comparison of a questioned hair or hairs from a crime scene with a known hair sample. A known hair sample consists of anywhere between 50 and 100 hairs from all portions of the area of interest, typically the head/scalp or pubic area. The hairs must be combed and pulled to collect both telogen and anagen hairs. A known sample must be representative of the collection area to be suitable for comparison purposes—braids, artificial treatment, graying, and other such characteristics must be noted and collected for a suitable known sample.

A comparison microscope is used for the examination. A comparison microscope is composed of two microscopes joined by an optical bridge to produce a split image. The sample on the right appears in the right-hand field of view and the sample on the left appears in the left-hand field of view. This side-by-side, point-by-point comparison is central to the effectiveness and accuracy of a forensic hair comparison. Hairs cannot be compared properly without one.

The hairs are examined from root to tip, at magnifications of 40× to 250×. Hairs are mounted on glass microscope slides with a mounting medium of an appropriate refractive index for hairs, about 1.5. All of the characteristics present are used and articulated in the following table. The known sample is characterized and described to capture its variety. The questioned hairs are then described individually. These descriptions cover the root, the microanatomy of the shaft, and the tip.

Three basic conclusions can be drawn from a forensic hair comparison. First, if the questioned hair exhibits the same microscopic characteristics as the known hair sample, then it could have come from the same person who provided the known sample. Hair comparisons are not a form of positive identification, however. Second, if the questioned hair

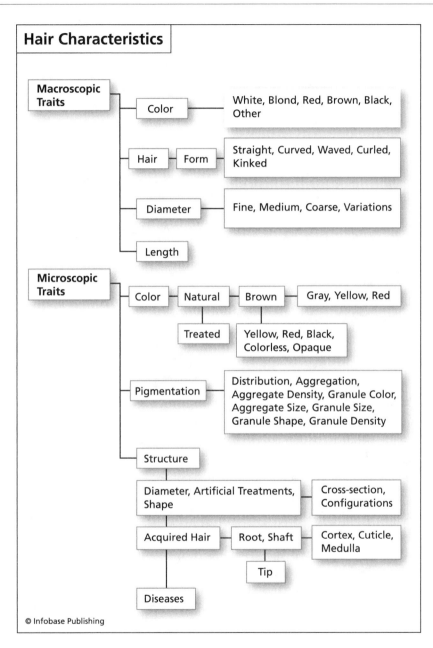

Hair Characteristics

Macroscopic Traits
- Color — White, Blond, Red, Brown, Black, Other
- Hair — Form — Straight, Curved, Waved, Curled, Kinked
- Diameter — Fine, Medium, Coarse, Variations
- Length

Microscopic Traits
- Color — Natural — Brown — Gray, Yellow, Red
  - Treated — Yellow, Red, Black, Colorless, Opaque
- Pigmentation — Distribution, Aggregation, Aggregate Density, Granule Color, Aggregate Size, Granule Size, Granule Shape, Granule Density
- Structure
  - Diameter, Artificial Treatments, Shape — Cross-section, Configurations
  - Acquired Hair — Root, Shaft — Cortex, Cuticle, Medulla
    - Tip
  - Diseases

© Infobase Publishing

exhibits similarities to and also slight differences from the known hair sample, then no conclusion can be drawn as to whether the questioned hair could have come from the known source. Finally, if the questioned hair exhibits different microscopic characteristics from the known hair sample, then it can be concluded that the questioned hair did not come from the known source.

The examination process must consider both the general traits and the types of variations found in the hairs that are compared. According to Dick Bisbing, a noted forensic hair expert, the decision-making process of a forensic hair comparison sums up this way:

> In order to conclude that a questioned hair is consistent with a known source, one must first determine that the characteristics exhibited by the questioned hair fit within the range of characteristics present in the known samples. Ideally, in order to strengthen the value of the hair association, the examiner must find a one-to-one correspondence between all characteristics of the questioned hair and one or two known hairs, with no significant differences over the length of the hair.

This evaluation and balancing of microscopic traits within and between samples is key to the comparison process.

STATISTICS AND HAIR EXAMINATIONS

Given the list of traits shown earlier, it might seem that hairs could be coded and entered into a database from which frequency information could eventually be derived. This would be of immense help in determining the significance of hairs as evidence. A hair's traits could be entered as a query and at the push of a button a frequency of occurrence for a population could be calculated. But it is not that easy.

Barry Gaudette, a former hair examiner with the Royal Canadian Mounted Police and a notable forensic hair examiner, enacted a clinical study in 1974 to attempt to determine the specificity of microscopic hair examinations. Gaudette's work coded and intercompared brown head hairs within European ancestry. The study determined that only 19 pairs of hairs were indistinguishable from each other, resulting in a frequency of one in 4,500 hairs. He did further work with pubic hairs in 1978 that resulted in a frequency of one in 1,600 pubic hairs.

Although critics complained that the 1974 study was flawed and the frequencies are not valid for any other sample, it was the first clinical study of its kind. Some examiners quoted these frequencies in their testimony to quantify the significance of their findings—a completely unjustified and erroneous application of the study. Statistics are used to describe general properties of collected data. The data collected by Gaudette was meant to demonstrate the usefulness of microscopical human hair comparisons in general, not in any one particular case. Just because Gaudette's work showed that one in 4,500 hairs in his study were indistinguishable does not mean than one in any 4,500 hairs are indistinguishable. Those data were not meant to be representative of the general population at large.

A later paper by one of Gaudette's colleagues elaborated on his study and refined the frequencies. Other, smaller studies provided additional insights into what the potential specificity of microscopic hair examinations might be. To date, however, no universal approach for calculating statistical significance has been published.

And none probably will be. Hairs are a very complicated composite biological material and the expression of hair traits across the population is highly variable. Being three-dimensional makes quantifying the traits that much more difficult. While a computer could be used to analyze digital images and categorize the hairs, a human could do it much faster and just as accurately. And now that DNA analysis is more accessible, this approach is hardly justified.

DNA AND HAIRS

DNA typing is an example of a revolutionary technology in the forensic and natural sciences. Advances in DNA analysis have not only allowed for personal identification from biological material, but has also greatly increased the kinds of biological material that can be analyzed. In the mid-1980s, Sir Alec Jeffreys developed the first effective method for isolating and comparing human DNA for forensic applications. This science has advanced to the point where forensic scientists are able to compare specific parts of the human genetic code.

DNA (deoxyribonucleic acid) is a molecule that is found in nearly all living cells; the only relevant exceptions are red blood cells and nerve cells. DNA is a special polymer; a polymer is a molecule made up of repeating simpler units, called monomers. Two types of DNA have forensic value: nuclear (also called genomic) and mitochondrial.

Nuclear (Genomic) DNA

A genomic DNA molecule can be thought of as a twisted ladder. The poles of the ladder are identical in all living things; they are made up of alternating sugar molecules (deoxyribose) and phosphates. Hanging from each sugar molecule is a "rung" made of two of four bases, called nucleotides: adenine (A), guanine (G), cytosine (C), and thymine (T). The two nucleotides that make up the "rung" are a bonded pair. When an adenine base and a thymine base come into proximity, they form a bond to each other. Likewise, when cytosine and guanine get near each other, they will bond. Thymine can only bond with adenine (and vice versa), while guanine can only bond with cytosine (and vice versa). The DNA molecule consists of the sugar-phosphate backbones connected by linked pairs of bases that can only be A-T, T-A, G-C, or C-G.

All the parts of DNA's structure described so far have been very predictable. The order in which the base pairs occur *along* the ladder, however, is not governed by similar rules—the pairs can occur in any order. The order of the base pairs constitutes a language of sorts, a genetic code for translating DNA into the characteristics of an organism. This small area of variability allows for a large array of unique combinations. These principles will be familiar to anyone who has used a telephone: Everyone has a 10-digit phone number (three-digit area code, three-digit exchange, and a four-digit number), but the digits must be dialed in the correct sequence to get to *you*.

From here on discussion will refer almost exclusively to humans. Most cells in the human body have a nucleus (not to be confused with the atomic nucleus) where most of the cell's functions are controlled. In humans the DNA in the nucleus is arranged into 46 structures called chromosomes. The chromosomes are arranged in 23 pairs; one member of each pair of chromosomes comes from the father and the other member comes from the mother. Male sperm contain 23 chromosomes and the female ovum (egg) also contains 23. When sperm and egg unite, the 23 chromosomes from the sperm and the egg pair up, forming the 46 found in every nucleated cell (cell with a nucleus) in the offspring. One pair of chromosomes determines the sex of the individual. For females, both chromosomes are of the X type. In males, one of the chromosomes is X and the other is Y.

Within the long strands of DNA are sections called genes. The base pair sequences in genes code for specific things; think of the base pairs as letters and the genes as words. The ordering of the base pairs in genes provides the chemical instructions to manufacture particular proteins in the body. Each gene codes for a particular characteristic protein. Perhaps surprisingly, more than 99 percent of all human DNA is exactly the same—it codes for the things that make us all human. The rest of the DNA (less than 1 percent) contains the genetic information that differentiates one human being from another.

Genes that determine a person's individual characteristics are found in particular locations on the chromosomes. Some traits are determined by a single gene on one chromosome. Others, such as eye color, are determined by multiple genes on several chromosomes. Simple observation of peoples' eyes indicates that there must be considerable variation in this gene—some people have brown eyes, others blue or green, and many have eye colors that are somewhere in between colors. For example, a person may inherit the eye color gene that codes for blue eyes from her mother and the same gene that codes for brown eyes from her father. The actual eye color that the child has is determined by genetic rules that can be complicated. The two different eye color genes are variants of the same gene (eye color); these variant types of genes are called alleles. If a person inherits the same form of a gene from the mother and the father, that person is said to be homozygous with respect to that gene.

Some characteristics exist in many forms, or alleles. Each person will inherit one allele from the mother and one from the father. If there are a large number of such alleles then there would be much variation among human beings at this location (or *locus,* Latin for "place"). This situation provides the basis for some kinds of DNA typing: The variation of alleles at several loci are exploited to divide a population into many subgroups. There may be so many of these subgroups that virtual individuality can be achieved.

An individual's genetic makeup is called the person's genotype, the genetic description of the individual's alleles. A person's genotype as expressed in a particular environment is called the phenotype. For example, a person's genotype may code for brown hair. If she lived in a city with little sunshine, where it was cloudy most of the time, her hair color would be expressed (phenotype) pretty much the way it was coded for genetically. But suppose she moved to a sunny, warm climate and got a job working outdoors. The Sun would bleach her hair and her phenotype would change; however, the genotype would not.

There are two types of variability in alleles. The first type is sequence polymorphisms (*poly* means "many" and *morph* means "shape"). An example of a sequence polymorphism in DNA would be:

```
CTCGATTAAGG CTCGGTTAAGG
GAGCTAATTCC GAGCCAATTCC
```

The two sequences of double stranded DNA are exactly the same except at the location indicated by underlining.

The other type of variation in DNA is called length polymorphism. Consider the following variations on a familiar song:

Happy birthday to you
Happy birthday to to you
Happy birthday to to to you
Happy birthday to to to to you

These phrases are all the same except for the word "to," which repeats a different number of times in the various phrases. Now consider the length polymorphism that occurs in the following DNA sequence:

```
CATGTAC-CATGTAC
GTACATG-GTACATG
CATGTAC-CATGTAC-CATGTAC-CATGTAC
GTACATG-GTACATG-GTACATG-GTACATG
```

Both DNA examples consist of a seven-base-pair sequence that is repeated. In the first case it is repeated twice. In the second example it is repeated four times. Because the repeats are next to each other, without any other base pairs in between, they are referred to as tandem repeats—like a tandem bicycle, where one seat is behind the other. If tandem repeats are found at the same locus in different people or in the same person, then this locus is described as having a variable number of tandem repeats (VNTR).

Most of the hairs found at crime scenes are not suitable for genomic DNA analysis. For a hair to be accessible for genomic DNA analysis, the root must have tissue attached to it. This is because genomic DNA is found only in nucleated cells, as explained earlier. Those hairs that are

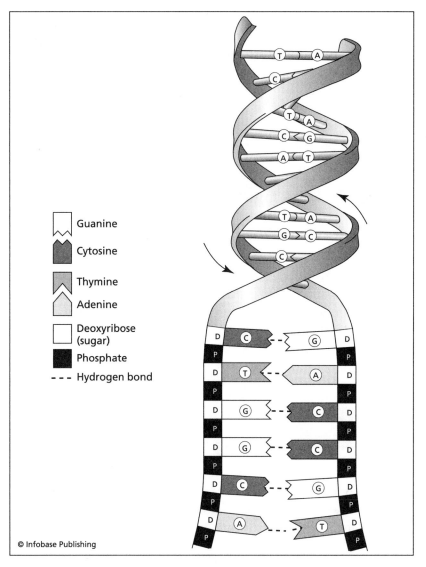

DNA is a fairly simple molecule made of four bases attached to a sugar and phosphate backbone

found with tissue attached to them are most often anagen (actively grow-ing) hairs, which were still connected to the hair follicle when removed. When an anagen hair is removed, part of the follicle is torn out with it, and this is the tissue that may yield useful DNA.

The hairs that are most often found are telogen (resting phase) hairs. These are the hairs people shed on a daily basis and whose loss signals the follicle to begin producing a hair again. Telogen hairs have roots that are dried and inactive—their connection to the follicle is only a thin tether at the base of the follicle. Recall that hairs are made of keratinized tissue. This renders any DNA in that tissue inert to genomic analysis methods.

Under the circumstances, it might seem that hairs are not very useful from a DNA point of view. In practice, however, hairs are very useful indeed, because they contain mitochondrial DNA.

Mitochondrial DNA (mtDNA)

Not all human DNA is located in the cell's nucleus. Just as bodies have organs, so do cells. The "organs" of cells are called organelles ("little organs"), and they exist in the cell but outside the nucleus. Some organ-elles have their own packets of DNA; one such organelle is the mitochon-drion (plural, mitochondria). Each cell contains several mitochondria, which function much like lungs—they help remove processed gases and waste. The proteins that control these functions are manufactured according to a genetic code, separate from that in the nucleus, that is housed within the mitochondria.

There are a number of differences between mitochondrial DNA (mtDNA) and genomic DNA.

- mtDNA is circular in shape, unlike the twisted ladder of ge-nomic DNA.

- mtDNA is shorter/smaller than genomic DNA, but thousands of copies of mtDNA exist in each mitochondrion. By contrast, there are only a few copies of genomic DNA in a human cell.

- mtDNA contains a noncoding region of only 1,100 base pairs (genomic DNA has many thousands of base pairs). This region does not code for any particular proteins; it just acts as a "spacer" for the sequence. Within this noncoding region are two areas that are extremely variable in their sequences (so-called hypervariable regions). During a cell's reproduction of DNA, certain base pairs will not be replicated exactly. Because they do not code for anything, such mutations do not harm the organism. But they mean that many differences will exist between mtDNA from two people with different mothers.

- All mtDNA comes from the mother; no mtDNA comes from the father. Barring mutations, every descendent of the same woman should have the same mtDNA. This makes mtDNA a very powerful tool for tracing family generations through the maternal side of the family.

- mtDNA often shows a high degree of variation between un-related people, making it a powerful tool in forensic typing. Although some sequences appear the same between people who are not maternally related, this is true of only a very, very small percentage of the population.

Mitochondrial DNA can be the last, best hope to identify people. A very hardy molecule, mtDNA survives in large quantities in hairs, bone, and teeth. The keratinization process does not affect the quality of mtDNA. Often, these sources are the only remains of individuals whose bodies are badly decomposed or who were victims of a mass disaster, like a plane crash or bombing. Not all forensic science laboratories that perform genomic DNA analysis also do mtDNA analysis. Those that do, however, generally use DNA sequencing; they determine the entire base pair sequence in the two hypervariable regions of the mtDNA, rather than relying on length polymorphism.

The advent of forensic mtDNA analysis in the mid-1990s heralded a new era of biological analysis in law enforcement. This was especially true for hairs, because mtDNA analysis offered a way to add informa-tion to microscopic hair examinations. The microscopic comparison of human hairs has been accepted scientifically and legally for decades. Mitochondrial DNA sequencing added another test for assessing the significance of attributing a hair to an individual.

The First Forensic Use of mtDNA

Mitochondrial DNA (mtDNA) evidence was introduced for the first time in a Tennessee murder prosecution against 27-year-old Paul Ware in September 1996. Ware was accused of the rape and murder of Lindsey Green, a four-year-old girl. The defendant claimed that another man in the home, a babysitter, had made it look as if Ware had committed the crime. Ware was found drunk and asleep next to the child's body. The victim's blood was not found on the suspect; the suspect's semen was not found on her. However, during the autopsy, a small red hair was discovered in the throat of the victim, and several small red hairs had been found in a bed at the crime scene.

Mitochondrial DNA was extracted from two of the hairs recovered from the crime scene, one from the throat of the victim and one from the bedsheet in the room where the rape was alleged to have occurred. Mitochondrial DNA was also extracted from a sample of Paul Ware's saliva and from the victim's blood. The mtDNA sequence from the hair in the throat and from the hair found on the sheet were compared and found to be exact mtDNA matches of each other. They were further compared to the saliva sample of the defendant and found to match. Each of these three mtDNA samples was compared to the known mtDNA sequence of the victim, and they did not match. Ware was convicted of murder and sentenced to life imprisonment.

Mitochondrial DNA is now routinely used in cases of criminal investigation, personal identity, and disaster-victim identification.

Neither the microscopic nor molecular analysis alone provides positive identification. Even combined, the two methods cannot provide positive identification. The two methods, however, complement each other in the information they provide. For example, mtDNA typing can often distinguish between hairs from different sources that have similar, or insufficient, microscopic hair characteristics, while hair comparisons with a microscope can often distinguish between samples from maternally related individuals—a situation where mtDNA analysis is "blind."

A study in 2000 demonstrated the strength of combining micro-scopic and mitochondrial examinations of human hairs. Of 170 hair examinations conducted by the FBI Laboratory, the study recorded 80 microscopic associations, of which only nine were excluded by mtDNA. The study also tracked 66 hairs that were subjected to mtDNA analy-sis; these hairs had not been identified through microscopic methods, either because they were considered unsuitable for microscopic exami-nation or because microscopy yielded inconclusive associations. Of the 66 hairs, only six failed to provide enough mtDNA, while another three yielded inconclusive results. In other words, by combining micro-scopic and mitochondrial methods, the FBI lab associated 128 out of 170 hairs in evidence. The data in the study support the usefulness of both methods.

It is important to be aware that microscopy and mtDNA analysis are not stratified tests; that is, one test is not better than the other. Rather, each analyzes different characteristics. Either or both methods can pro-vide important information to an investigation. The only question left, then, is the order in which to run the tests. James Robertson of the Aus-tralian Federal Police suggests that microscopy should come first, for the sake of practicality: "It will be both necessary and desirable to eliminate as many questioned hairs as possible and concentrate mtDNA analysis on only key hairs." Consequently, Robertson predicts that there will be "little if any reduction" in how much microscopic examination labs will need to do. The need for both methods is echoed in the expanding use of both microscopical and mitochondrial DNA examinations of hairs in forensic cases.

4

Fibers

Textile fibers are one of the most frequently encountered types of physical evidence. Textiles are found in homes, offices, and vehicles. Fibers from textiles in these environments are constantly shed and transferred to people, places, and other objects. Some are better "shedders," such as fuzzy sweaters, than others—a tightly woven dress shirt, for example. Certain textiles also retain fibers better than others, depending on their construction, purpose, use, and other factors, like how often they are cleaned.

Fibers are also one of the most neglected and undervalued kinds of forensic evidence. Fibers provide many qualitative and quantitative traits for comparison. Textile fibers are often produced with specific end-use products in mind (underwear made from carpet fibers would be very uncomfortable), and these end uses lead to a variety of discrete traits designed into the fibers.

Color is another powerful discriminating characteristic. About 7,000 commercial dyes and pigments are used to color textiles; no single dye is used to create any particular color; and millions of shades of colors are possible in textiles. It is rare to find two fibers at random that exhibit the same microscopic characteristics and optical properties, especially color.

Applying statistical methods to trace evidence is difficult, however, because of a lack of fundamental information about how much of any kind of item exists. Very often, even the company that made a particular fiber will not know how many products those fibers went into. Forensic scientists try to estimate the frequency of textiles in populations; for example, calculating from databases in Germany and England, the chance of finding a woman's blouse made of turquoise acetate fibers among a random population of garments was estimated to be nearly four in 1 million. Famous cases, such as the trial of Wayne Williams in Atlanta, Georgia, or of O. J. Simpson in Los Angeles, California, also demonstrate the usefulness of forensic textile fiber analysis in demonstrating probative associations in criminal investigations.

TEXTILE FIBERS

A textile fiber is a unit of matter, either natural or manufactured, that has a length at least 100 times its diameter and forms the basic element of fabrics and other textiles. Fibers differ from each other in their chemical nature, cross-sectional shape, surface contour, and color, as well as length and diameter.

Fibers are classified as either natural or manufactured. A natural fiber is any fiber that exists as a fiber in its natural state. A manufactured fiber is any fiber derived from any substance that, at any point in the manufacturing process, is not a fiber. Fibers can also be designated by their chemical makeup as either protein, cellulosic, mineral, or synthetic. Protein fibers are composed of polymers of amino acids. Cellulosic fibers, by contrast, are made of polymers formed from carbohydrates. Mineral (inorganic) fibers may be composed of silica obtained from rocks or sand, while synthetic fibers are made of polymers that originate from small organic molecules that combine with water and air.

The generic names for manufactured and synthetic fibers were established as part of the Textile Fiber Products Identification Act enacted by Congress in 1954. In 1996, lyocell, discovered in 1988, was named as a new, subgeneric class of rayon.

FEDERAL TRADE COMMISSION TEXTILE PRODUCTS IDENTIFICATION ACT DEFINITIONS

acetate   a manufactured fiber in which the fiber-forming substance is cellulose acetate; where not less than 92 percent of the hydroxyl groups are acetylated, the term *triacetate* may be used as a generic description of the fiber

acrylic   a manufactured fiber in which the fiber-forming substance is any long-chain synthetic polymer composed of at least 85 percent by weight of acrylonitrile units

anidex   a manufactured fiber in which the fiber-forming substance is any long-chain synthetic polymer composed of at least 50 percent by weight of one or more esters of a monohydric alcohol and acrylic acid

aramid   a manufactured fiber in which the fiber-forming substance is any long-chain synthetic polyamide in which at least 85 percent of the amide linkages are attached directly to two aromatic rings

glass   a manufactured fiber in which the fiber-forming substance is glass

lyocell   a manufactured fiber composed of precipitated cellulose and produced by a solvent extrusion process where no chemical intermediates are formed

metallic   a manufactured fiber composed of metal, plastic-coated metal, metal-coated plastic, or a core completely covered by metal

modacrylic   a manufactured fiber in which the fiber-forming substance is any long-chain synthetic polymer composed of less than 85 percent but at least 35 percent by weight of acrylonitrile units

nylon   a manufactured fiber in which the fiber-forming substance is a long-chain synthetic polyamide in which less than 85 percent of the amide linkages are attached directly to two aromatic rings

The diameter of textile fibers is relatively small, generally 0.0004 to 0.002 inches (10 to 5 μm). Their length can vary from about 0.875 inches (2.2 cm) to, literally, miles. Based on length, fibers are classified as either filament or staple fiber. Filaments are a type of fiber having indefinite or extreme length, such as silk or a manufactured fiber. Staple fibers are

nytril	a manufactured fiber in which the fiber-forming substance is any long-chain synthetic polymer composed of at least 85 percent of a long-chain polymer of vinylidene dinitrile where the vinylidene dinitrile content is no less than every other unit in the polymer chain
olefin	a manufactured fiber in which the fiber-forming substance is any long-chain synthetic polymer composed of at least 85 percent by weight of ethylene, propylene, or other olefin units
polyester	a manufactured fiber in which the fiber-forming substance is any long-chain synthetic polymer composed of at least 85 percent by weight of an ester of a substituted aromatic carboxylic acid, including but not restricted to substituted terephthalate units and para-substituted hydroxybenzoate units
rayon	a manufactured fiber composed of regenerated cellulose, as well as manufactured fibers composed of regenerated cellulose in which substituents have replaced not more than 15 percent of the hydrogens of the hydroxyl groups
saran	a manufactured fiber in which the fiber-forming substance is any long-chain synthetic polymer composed of at least 80 percent by weight of vinylidene chloride units
spandex	a manufactured fiber in which the fiber-forming substance is any long-chain synthetic polymer composed of at least 85 percent of a segmented polyurethane
vinal	a manufactured fiber in which the fiber-forming substance is any long-chain synthetic polymer composed of at least 50 percent by weight of vinyl alcohol units and in which the total of the vinyl alcohol units and any one or more of the various acetal units is at least 85 percent by weight of the fiber
vinyon	a manufactured fiber in which the fiber-forming substance is any long-chain synthetic polymer composed of at least 85 percent by weight of vinyl chloride units

natural fibers (other than silk) or cut lengths of filament, typically 0.875 to 8 inches (2.2 to 20.3 cm) in length.

The size of natural fibers is usually given as a diameter measurement in micrometers (μm). The size of silk and manufactured fibers is usually given in denier (in the United States) or tex (in other countries).

Wallace Carothers (1896–1937): Notable Chemist and Inventor

Born on April 27, 1896, Wallace Carothers was an American chemist and the leader of organic chemistry at DuPont and is credited with the invention of nylon.

After earning a bachelor's degree in 1921 from the University of Illinois, Carothers went to the University of South Dakota, where he began his independent research at the same time he was a chemistry instructor. He earned a Ph.D. from the University of Illinois in 1924 with a specialty in organic chemistry. Carothers then worked at the University of Illinois for two years before going to Harvard University in 1926 to teach organic chemistry. In 1927, the DuPont Company made the radical decision to fund a unit that performed fundamental research—that is, research not focused on producing a marketable product. Carothers was considered for the position of heading up the laboratory. Initially Carothers declined the position, but was convinced by DuPont to accept the job and started in 1928.

Carothers assembled an impressive team of chemists, including some of his former teachers from the University of Illinois. In 1930, with new management of the laboratory, the group isolated chloroprene, a solid material that resembled rubber. This product, known as neoprene, was the first synthetic rubber. Additional research successes followed as did personal failures for Carothers. He had been plagued with depression his entire life and even spent time in a clinic. Carothers returned to DuPont after his treatment and began work on polyamides. In 1935, a half-ounce of a polymer, which was called polyamide 6,6 because of its arrangement of six carbon atoms side by side, was produced. Eventually, other types of this polyamide, dubbed nylon, would be produced, each specified by its arrangement of carbon atoms.

In 1936, Carothers was elected to the National Academy of Sciences, the first industrial organic chemist to receive this honor. Carothers was unhappy with his life's work, constantly battled depression, and felt that he had not accomplished much in his career. He committed suicide on April 29, 1937, mourning the recent death of his favorite sister.

Glass fibers are the only manufactured fibers that are not measured by denier.

Denier and tex are linear measurements based on weight per unit length. (The denier is the weight in grams of 9,000 meters of the fibers material.) Denier is a direct numbering system in which the lower numbers represent the finer sizes and the higher numbers the larger sizes. The denier system does not, however, record differences in density. For instance, a 1 denier nylon fiber is not equal in size to a 1 denier rayon fiber, because the fibers differ in density. Tex is equal to the weight in grams of 1,000 meters (1 km) of the fibrous material. To convert from tex to denier, divide the tex value by 0.1111; to convert from denier to tex, multiply the denier value by 0.1111.

THE COMPOSITION OF FIBERS

All fibers, natural or manufactured, are chain-like macromolecules called polymers, with hundreds or thousands of repeating chemical units called monomers linked together. Three polymer types occur in textile fibers: homopolymers, in which one monomer repeats itself along the polymer chain; copolymers, in which two or more monomers compose the polymer chain; and block polymers, where blocks of homopolymers are repeated along the chain. The three types of polymers are shown in the illustration.

Natural Fibers

The first textiles were made of natural fibers. Currently, more than half of the fibers produced each year are natural fibers and the majority of these are cotton. In fact, about half of all fibers produced annually are cotton. Natural fibers come from animals, plants, or minerals and are used in many products. It is important for the forensic fiber examiner to have a thorough knowledge of natural fibers and their significance in casework.

Animal fibers come from either mammals (hairs) or certain invertebrates, such as the silkworm. Animal fibers in textiles are most often from wool-bearing animals, such as sheep and goats, or from fur-bearing animals, like rabbits, mink, and fox. A comprehensive reference collection is critical to animal-hair identifications and comparisons. The

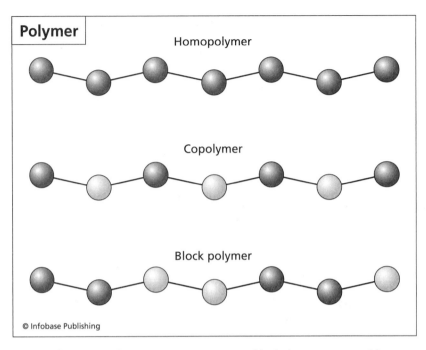

Homopolymers are the most common type and include acetate, aramid, cotton, nylon, olefin, PBI, polyester, rayon, silk, sulfar, triacetate, and wool. The fiber types that contain copolymers are acrylic, modacrylic, saran, and vinyon; the number and type of comonomers help to identify the specific fiber subtype. Spandex is an example of a block polymer fiber.

microscopic anatomical structures of animal hairs are important to their identification.

The three major sources for fibers derived from plants are the seed, the stem (bast fibers), and the leaf. Which source is used depends upon which source in a particular plant works best. Plant fibers are used in two principal forms: the technical fiber, used in cordage, sacks, mats, and the like; and individual cells (ultimates), used in fabrics and paper. Ultimates are the individual fibers, like cotton fibers, that make finer yarns and textiles. Separated from the other ultimates, the internal characteristics of each fiber are easier to see. Two of these characteristics that are specific to plant materials are the lumen and dislocations. The lumen is a central canal running along the length of the fiber; the lumen is part of the circulatory system of the plant. Dislocations are just that—cracks or fissures that appear in the middle of the fiber as diagonal or crossed fault lines. A forensic analyst's examination of technical fibers should include a search for internal structures and the preparation of a cross section. In preparation for the examination of ultimates, technical fibers should be mashed, fabrics teased apart, and paper repulped. The relative thickness of the cell walls; the size, shape, and thickness of the lumen (plural, *lumina*); cell length; and the presence, type, and distribution of dislocations should be noted. The most common plant fibers encountered in casework are cotton, flax, jute, hemp, ramie, sisal, abaca, coir, and kapok.

Mineral fibers are typically found as either asbestos fibers (natural) or as glass fibers (manufactured). These fibers are not used in textiles but appear in other products, such as fiberglass or composite materials. Because of health concerns, asbestos is rarely used for any products.

Manufactured Fibers

Manufactured fibers are the various families of fibers produced from fiber-forming substances, which may be synthesized polymers, modified or transformed natural polymers, or glass. Synthetic fibers are manufactured fibers synthesized from chemical compounds, such as nylon or polyester. Therefore, all synthetic fibers are manufactured, but not all manufactured fibers are synthetic. Manufactured fibers differ physically in their shape, size, internal properties, and appearance. The microscopic characteristics of manufactured fibers are the basic features used to distinguish them.

The bonding of monomers to form polymers is a chemical process called polymerization. The chemical reactions that build polymers for synthetic manufactured fibers occur by either of two mechanisms: condensation and addition.

In a condensation reaction, each bond that forms involves the release of water or some other simple substance, such as ethylene glycol in polyester production. Condensation reactions yield a product in which the repeating unit has fewer atoms than the monomer or monomers.

In an addition reaction, the resulting polymer consists of subunits whose molecular formulae are identical to those of the monomer. The monomers are combined, like links in a chain, to create longer polymers.

The Development of Synthetic Fibers

The desire to manufacture fibers derives from a need for control. Natural fibers and natural dyes all vary in their quality, and the combination of this variation leads to unsatisfactory reproducibility for textile manufacturers. While the search for a controlled method of producing fibers began long ago, the first artificial fiber was produced about 1855 by Georges Audemars. Nitrocellulose is soluble in organic solvents, like ether or acetone, which made it possible to develop the first manufactured fiber, called artificial silk. Audemars's method, however, could not be used for commercial production. Hilaire de Charbonnet patented a process for a celluosic fiber in 1884 and commercial production started 1891. The fiber was flammable and costly; production was stopped before World War I.

In 1894, another celluosic fiber was patented, which was named viscose, because the reaction product was a highly viscous solution. Avtex Fibers Incorporated began selling the fiber in 1910 in the United States. The trade name rayon was adopted in 1924; the name viscose was thereafter used for the viscous liquid used to make both rayon and cellophane. In Europe, however, the fiber and fabric became known as viscose, and is still referred to that way.

The next big advance in manufactured fiber discovery did not occur until nylon was created by DuPont. Nylon first appeared commercially in a nylon-bristled toothbrush in 1938; its use in a textile was made famous by using it in women's "nylons" (stockings) in 1940. Nylon, a polymer, is made of repeating units (or monomers) linked by peptide bonds (also called amide bonds); nylon is referred to as a polyamide. Nylon was the first commercially successful polymer and the first synthetic fiber to be made entirely from coal, water, and air. Like most manufactured fibers, nylon was intended to be a replacement for silk; it was used in parachutes, ropes, flak vests, tires, combat uniforms and other military uses after the United States entered World War II in 1941. Type nylon 6,6 is the most common commercial grade of nylon. With the 1950s being the heyday for fiber discovery, other fiber types followed, including acrylic (1950), polyester (1953), olefin (1958), spandex (1959), and lyocell (1988).

The molecular weight of the polymer is the sum of the molecular weight of all of the monomers in the chain.

Synthetic fibers are formed by extrusion. The fiber-forming substance, called spinning dope, is extruded through a hole or holes in a device called a spinneret, which is comparable to a showerhead. This process is called spinning. The spinning dope consists of a monomeric material that is initially solid. It is rendered into a liquid or semiliquid form by a solvent or heat.

After the fibers are spun, they may go through a number of steps before they are ready for construction into yarns or shipment as fibers. Fibers are typically drawn (stretched out) to increase their length, strength, and form; drawing a fiber affects its optical properties. The spun fibers may also be treated with chemicals to yield a desired property, such as increased apparel comfort or stain-resistance. Finally, synthetic fibers may be crimped to alter their physical form.

TEXTILE CONSTRUCTION

Yarn is a term for continuous strands of textile fibers, filaments, or material in a form suitable for weaving, knitting, or otherwise entangling to form a textile fabric. Yarns may be constructed to have an S-twist (clockwise), a Z-twist (counterclockwise), or no twist at all (zero twist). These terms come from the orientation of the middle bar of the two letters (that is, "\" or "/") and describe the directionality of the yarn's twist. A yarn may be constructed as a number of smaller single yarns twisted together to form a plied yarn; each ply will have its own twist as well as the overall twist of the plied yarn. Do not confuse the terms *yarn* and *thread*: Thread refers to the product used to join pieces of fabric together, typically by sewing, while yarn is the product used to make fabric.

Fabric is a textile structure produced by interlacing yarns, fibers, or filaments with a substantial surface area relative to their thickness. Fabrics are defined by their method of assembly. The three major types of fabrics are woven, knitted, and nonwoven.

Woven Fabrics

Fabrics have been woven since the dawn of civilization. Woven fabrics are those fabrics composed of two sets of yarns, called warp and weft, and are formed by the interlacing of these sets of yarns. The way these sets of

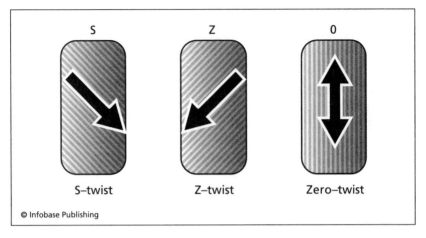

S   Z   0

S–twist   Z–twist   Zero–twist

© Infobase Publishing

Yarns may be constructed to have a S-twist (clockwise), a Z-twist (counterclockwise), or a zero-twist (no twist at all). These terms come from the orientation of the middle bar of the two letters and describe the directionality of the yarn's twist.

yarns are interlaced determines the weave. Warp yarns run lengthwise in the fabric and weft yarns run crosswise; weft may also be referred to as filling, woof, or picks. An almost unlimited variety of constructions can be fashioned by weaving.

Knitted Fabrics

Knitted fabrics are constructed of interlocking series of loops of one or more yarns. There are two major categories of knit fabrics: warp knitting and weft knitting. In warp knits the yarns generally run lengthwise in the fabric, whereas in weft knits the yarns generally run crosswise to the fabric. The basic components of a knit fabric are courses, which are rows of loops across the width of the fabric, and wales, which are rows of loops along the length of the fabric. Unlike woven fabrics, in which warp and weft are made up of different sets of yarns, the courses and wales of knit fabrics are formed by a single yarn.

Nonwoven Fabrics

Nonwoven fabrics are an assembly of textile fibers held together without weaving or knitting. The fibers may be held together by mechanical interlocking in a random web or mat, by fusing of the fibers, or by bonding with a cementing medium. Felt, the first fabric ever made from wool, is a good example. Wet wool fibers are passed through rollers to press them together into a mat; the mat is rerolled to flatten it further and then allowed to dry. Once it is dry, it creates a soft but weak fabric. A wide variety of nonwoven construction methods are currently in use, however, and other examples are bandage pads, automotive textiles, and medical fabrics.

ANALYSIS OF FIBERS

The shape of fibers plays a role in their identification. Natural fibers are used for products such as cordage and rugs, more often than they are used in other products. Manufactured fibers are made with particular end uses in mind. Beyond fiber size and type, many other traits serve to differentiate textile fibers.

Crimp is the waviness of a fiber, expressed as crimps per unit length. Crimp may be two-dimensional or three-dimensional in nature. Some fibers are naturally crimped, like wool, while others are more linear, such as silk. Crimp must be added to manufactured fibers.

Makers introduce color to manufactured fibers using dyes or pigments. Natural fibers, which may be white, off-white, or a shade of brown, can be bleached to remove any natural color so they may be dyed more easily. The color of a fiber may vary along its length due to inconsistent uptake of dye or because the color has been printed (inconsistently) onto the fabric, rather than dyed. All of these traits should be noted in forensic analysis.

Optical properties, such as refractive index, birefringence, and color, are traits that relate to a fiber's structure or treatment. Some of these characteristics help forensic analysts to identify the generic polymer class of manufactured fibers. Others, such as color, are critical indicators of fibers that have been dyed or chemically finished. A visual and analytical assessment of fiber color must be part of every fiber comparison. The fluorescence of fibers and their dyes is another useful point of comparison.

Thermal properties relate to the softening and melting temperatures for manufactured fibers and the changes the fiber exhibits when heated. Since synthetic fibers are essentially plastic, they will soften or melt at

MELTING TEMPERATURES FOR SOME FIBER TYPES

Fiber Type	Temperature (C°)
acetate	224–280
acrylic	does not melt
aramid	does not melt
modacrylic*	204–225
nylon	
6	213
6,12	217–227
6,6	254–267

Note: * some members of this class do not melt

specific temperatures based on their chemistry. Thermal testing should be considered last as it is a destructive test.

Based on its polymer composition, a fiber will react differently to various instrumental methods, such as Fourier transform—infrared spectroscopy (FT-IR) or pyrolysis–gas chromatography (P-GC), and to various chemicals, such as acids or bases. These reactions yield information about the fiber's molecular structure and composition.

MICROSCOPIC CHARACTERISTICS

A polarized light microscope is the primary tool for the identification and analysis of manufactured fibers. Many characteristics of manufactured fibers can be viewed in nonpolarized light, however, and these provide a fast, direct, and accurate method for the discrimination of similar fibers. To confirm whether the known and the questioned fibers truly present the same microscopic characteristics, the analyst must use a comparison light microscope.

The way a fiber's diameter is measured is dependent upon its cross-sectional shape. If a fiber is circular in cross section, it is easy to measure its diameter. There is more than one way to measure the diameter of a

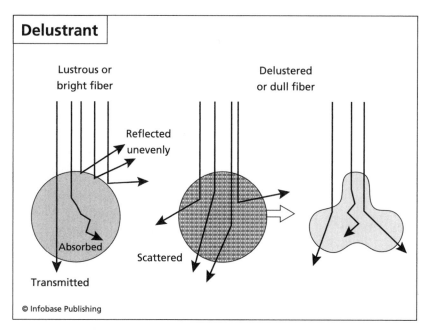

Delustrant

Lustrous or bright fiber

Delustered or dull fiber

Reflected unevenly

Absorbed

Scattered

Transmitted

© Infobase Publishing

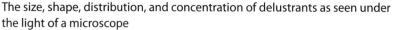

The size, shape, distribution, and concentration of delustrants as seen under the light of a microscope

non-round fiber, however. Manufactured fibers can be made in diameters from as small as 6 μm (so-called microfibers) up to almost any size, because diameter size is limited only by the width of the spinneret holes. By comparison, natural fibers vary in diameter from cultivated silk (10 to 13 μm) to U.S. sheep's wool (up to 40 μm or more), while human scalp hairs range from 50 to 100 μm in diameter.

Delustrants are finely ground particles of materials, such as titanium dioxide, that are introduced into the spinning dope. These particles help to diffract light passing through the fibers and reduce their luster. The size, shape, distribution, and concentration of delustrants should be noted.

OPTICAL PROPERTIES OF MANUFACTURED FIBERS

The optical properties of manufactured fibers can yield a tremendous amount of information about their chemistry, production, end use, and environment. Careful measurement and analysis of these properties are a crucial step in the identification and later comparison of textile fibers.

Polarized Light Microscopy

Polarized light microscopy is an easy and quick nondestructive way to determine the generic polymer class of manufactured and synthetic textile fibers. Beyond the immediate characteristics used to discriminate between polymer types, the examination of fibers in polarized light provides valuable information about the production and finishing of the fiber after spinning.

Fluorescence Microscopy

Many dyes used to color textiles have fluorescent components, and their response to certain wavelengths of light can be useful in comparing textile fibers. Not all textile dyes fluoresce, but fluorescence comparisons should be performed regardless: If the questioned and known fibers both fail to fluoresce, that is another point of meaningful comparison.

Fluorescence occurs when a substance is excited by specific wavelengths of light. A light of relatively short wavelength illuminates a substance and the substance absorbs and/or converts a certain, small part of the light (into heat, for example). Most of the light that is not absorbed by the substance is reemitted as fluorescence. The fluorescent light has lost some of its energy and its wavelength will be longer than that of the source light.

Certain dye combinations may produce fluorescence of a particular intensity and color, both of which should be noted during the examination. Fibers colored with similar dyes should exhibit the same fluorescence characteristics, unless the fiber and/or dye(s) have been degraded (such as by UV exposure or bleaching). It is important to consider these factors when collecting known samples.

COLOR MEASUREMENT

Color is one of the most critical characteristics in a fiber comparison. Almost all manufacturing industries are concerned with product appearance. Everything that is manufactured has a color, and often these colors are imparted to the end product. Particular colors are chosen for some products rather than others (it is difficult to find "safety orange" carpeting, for example) and these colors may indicate the end product. The number of producible colors is nearly infinite and color is an easy discriminator.

More than 80 dyers worldwide and almost 350 trademarked dyes are registered with the American Association of Textile Chemists and Colorists (AATCC), a body that seeks to promote the increase of knowledge of the application of colorants, chemicals, and polymers in the textile industry. Some trademarked dyes have as many as 40 variants, and more than 7,000 dyes and pigments are currently produced worldwide. Natural dyes, such as indigo, have been known since prehistory, while synthetic dyes have gained prominence largely since World War I.

A dye is an organic chemical that is able to absorb and reflect certain wavelengths of visible light. Pigments are microscopic, water-insoluble particles that are either incorporated into the fiber at the time of production or are bonded to the surface of the fiber by a resin. Some fiber types, such as olefins, are not easily dyed and therefore are often pigmented.

Based upon the desired end product effects, the fiber substrate, and the type of dye used, there are more than 12 different application categories for textile dyes. Very few textiles are colored with only one dye and even a simple dye may be put through eight to ten processing steps to achieve a final dye form, shade, and strength. When all of these factors are considered, it becomes apparent that it is virtually impossible to dye textiles in a continuous method; that is, dyeing separate batches of fibers or textiles is the rule rather than the exception. This color variability has the potential to be significant in forensic fiber comparisons. The three main methods of analyzing the color in fibers are visual examination, chemical analysis, and instrumental analysis. Each of these methods has strengths and weaknesses that the fiber examiner must consider. The most basic method is simple visual examination of single fibers with the aid of a comparison microscope. Visual examination and comparison is quick and comparison is an excellent screening technique. However, it is a subjective method, and because of day-to-day and observer-to-observer variations, it is not

Discovery of Synthetic Dyes

In 1853, William Henry Perkin entered the Royal College of Chemistry in London (now part of Imperial College London), where he began his studies in chemistry at 15 years old. The chemistry that Perkin studied was primitive, at best. Atomic theory was accepted but, while the proportions of elements could be determined, the arrangement of the elements in compounds was difficult to figure out. Perkin worked to synthesize quinine, an expensive natural product used to treat malaria. During a holiday break in 1856 when his supervisor was away, Perkin tried some experiments in his apartment, where he had set up a crude laboratory. Like many great discoveries, Perkin's initial work failed to achieve his desired result—aniline, a cousin to quinine, could be produced but resulted in a sticky substance that stained whatever it touched a deep purple. Intrigued, Perkin worked on his own time (it was not what he had been assigned to do at work) to conduct further experiments.

Perkin determined that the material, which he called mauveine after the deep purple color, could be manufactured reliably and commercially. It dyed silk wonderfully and did not fade. He filed for a patent for mauveine later in 1856; he was just 18. Until then, all textile dyes were produced from natural products and were expensive, laborious

always a repeatable method. Additionally, the dilemma of metameric colors exists. Metameric colors are those that appear to match in one set of lighting conditions but not in another. By their nature, metamers are difficult to sort out visually. Visual examination must be used in conjunction with an objective method.

The perception of color by a human observer is subject to a variety of factors, including genetics, age, and environment. The human visual system is complex and adaptive. The phenomenon called simultaneous contrast is the perception of color based on context. Another example of contextual color perception is known as the chameleon effect, where to produce, and unpredictable in their quality. Purple, for example, had always come from glands of shellfish; it would take thousands of the creatures to dye one or two garments. Tyrian purple, as it was known, was reserved for the rich and the royal. Perkin understood that mauveine had significant commercial possibilities. Perkin solved many business and technological challenges, and mauveine became a tremendous commercial success, making Perkin very rich.

Perkin's discovery came at just the right time—the beginning of the Industrial Revolution. His success demonstrated that science and business were not mutually exclusive. Many scientists at that time felt that anything that smacked of making money was beneath them and they were concerned solely with academia. By making mauveine work chemically and profitably, Perkin showed that good chemistry could mix with good business. Many new aniline dyes appeared in the following years, some created by Perkin. Factories sprouted all across Europe to produce the new dyes.

Perkin received many honors in his lifetime, including the Royal Society's Royal Medal. The Perkin Medal was established in 1906 to commemorate the 50th anniversary of the discovery of mauveine and is the highest honor in American industrial chemistry. Perkin died in 1907.

colors change based upon the surrounding colors. Because of the factors influencing human color perception, any visual comparison must be checked by an objective method of color measurement.

Chemical analysis involves extracting the dye and characterizing or identifying its chemistry. Typically, thin-layer chromatography (TLC) is the method of choice. Chemical analysis addresses the type of dye or dyes used to color the fiber and may help to sort out metameric colors. It can be difficult to extract the dye from the fiber, however, because forensic samples typically are small and textile dyers take great pains to ensure that the dye stays in the fiber. Dye analysis is also a destructive

The microspectrophotometer (MSP) in the UV/vis range is an instrument that allows for the color measurement of individual fibers. The MSP is essentially a standard spectrophotometer with a microscope attached to focus on the sample. The photograph is that of a QDI 2010™ microspectrometer, which incorporates the latest technological advances in optics, spectroscopy, and software. *(Craic Technologies)*

method, rendering the fiber useless for further color analysis. In addition, dye analysis of very light or very small fibers may result in weak or equivocal responses, because such fibers contain little dye.

Instrumental analysis offers the best combinations of strengths and the fewest weaknesses of the three methods. Instrumental readings are objective and repeatable; the results are quantitative; and the methods can be standardized. Importantly, instrumental analysis is not destructive to the fiber and it may be repeated. Again, very light-colored fibers may present a problem with weak results and natural fibers may exhibit high variations due to uneven dye uptake.

The microspectrophotometer (MSP) in the UV/vis range is an instrument that allows for the color measurement of individual fibers. The MSP is essentially a standard spectrophotometer with a microscope attached to focus on the sample. A spectrophotometer compares the amount of light passing through air with the amount of light transmitted through or reflected off of a sample. The ratio of these measurements indicates the percentage of light reflected or transmitted. At each wavelength of the visible spectrum, this ratio is calculated, stored, and recorded. The light is broken into smaller regions of the visible spectrum by a monochromator, which acts like a prism dividing the light into its spectral components.

Color is a major factor in comparing textile fibers. If one is searching tape lifts, it is the predominant factor in selecting fibers for further comparison. Very fine gradations of color difference can be seen once fibers have been mounted; it is necessary, however, to train the observer's eye to make these distinctions in a uniform manner. The microspectrophotometer is crucial to the comparison process because it can segregate colored fibers that appear visually the same but are subtly different. Objectively distinguishing between otherwise identical fibers is necessary to ensure a reliable comparison method.

CHEMICAL PROPERTIES

While microscopy offers an accurate method of fiber examination, it is often necessary to confirm these observations. Analyzing the fibers chemically offers not only a confirmation of the microscopic work but may also provide additional information about the specific polymer type or types that make up the fiber. Many types of synthetic fibers have more than one "flavor," so to speak. For example, nylon has about a dozen subtypes which are defined by the chemical structure: nylon 6 has a row of six carbon atoms while nylon 6,6 has two rows of six carbon atoms. Fourier transform–infrared spectroscopy (FT-IR) and pyrolysis–gas chromatography (P-GC) are both methods of assessing the chemical structure of polymers. FT-IR is the preferred method because it is not destructive of the fibers.

Manufactured fibers also can be characterized by their reaction to certain chemicals. Prior to the introduction of instrumentation in crime laboratories, this was a popular method. Solubility analysis lacks the specificity of instrumental methods and is destructive, but it can still be an effective means to confirm a manufactured fiber's generic class.

Solubility tests should be performed on both the known and questioned fibers side-by-side, either on spot plate or on a microscope slide with a coverslip. A hot-stage microscope may be required for some methods. Numerous solubility procedures exist, and one should be chosen with available chemicals, equipment, and safety in mind.

INTERPRETATIONS

What does a positive fiber association mean? Numerous studies have shown that, other than white cotton, indigo-dyed cotton (denim), and certain types of black cotton, no fiber should be regarded as "common." These studies include looking for specific fibers on a wide variety of clothing, cross-checking fibers in particular locations (movie theater seats, for example). One study cross-checked fibers from 20 unrelated cases, looking for incidental positive associations; in more than 2 million comparisons, no incidental positive associations were found. This makes fiber evidence very powerful in demonstrating associations.

The ultimate goal of all forensic evidence analysis is to be able to identify a piece of physical evidence with a source (person, place, or object) to the exclusion of all other similar objects. Evidence of this type is said to be individual. Evidence classified as individual is posited to possess unique characteristics not possessed by other members of the same type of evidence. For example, if a piece of glass is broken into three pieces and they are reconstructed such that they all fit together, the set of objects from which those pieces could have originated contains one, and only one, member.

By contrast, class evidence cannot be definitively associated with only one source to the exclusion of all others. While this statement seems to contradict the premise that all items are unique in time and/or space, what it really meant is that class evidence lacks sufficient distinguishing characteristics to be individualized. It is not possible, for example, to tell the difference chemically or optically between two adjacent fibers taken from the same shirt. We know through simple observation that the two fibers came from the same shirt but we cannot prove this to someone who did not see us remove the fibers. By any test we devise, the two fibers and the rest of the fibers in the shirt will yield the same analytical results. Those fibers are different, however, from fibers comprising many, many other shirts; in fact, it is rare to find two fibers at random that exhibit all the same microscopic characteristics and optical properties.

Positive associations between items of class evidence are often expressed as one of the following three stated conclusions (or variations on one of the following):

- the questioned item *could have* originated from the same source as the known item

- the known source *could not be eliminated* as the source of the questioned item

- the questioned item is *consistent with* originating from the same source as the known item

In other words, there is a sliding scale of specificity for class evidence based on the number of hierarchical categories into which a particular item can be placed.

For fibers, this may be due in large part to the number of analyses carried out and, therefore, the number of features that are common to both known and questioned fibers. In target fiber studies, textiles, typically from casework or public sources, are chosen and specific fiber types are targeted. Then the textiles are examined to see if any of the targeted fibers are present and, if so, how many. The first target fiber study was performed in 1941. One hundred ninety-three bolts of cloth used for making men's suits were used to provide 26 distinct types of blue fibers to act as target fibers. Testers then examined the bolts of cloth to see how many colors of the blue fibers were present. They found that less than 6 percent of any one color matched the cloths, basing their comparisons only on the results of comparison microscopy. A similar study was performed in 1952 using other colors of wool fibers. They vacuumed the clothing of 35 persons and checked for coincidental matches; these occurred only in 1 percent of the cases, using only comparison microscopy.

In a more extensive 1986 study, the Metropolitan Police Forensic Science Laboratory in London (now the Forensic Science Service) carried out a target fiber study using four popular garments sold in Britain. They examined tapings taken from 250 casework samples over a one-year period to see how many fibers were found matching those from any of the four garments. Fibers matching those from only one of the four garments were found on only four tapings and no more than two target fibers were found on any one taping. Similar results were obtained in another study using two target fibers—red wool and brown polyester. The front seats of 108 motor vehicles were examined. Out of more than 8,000 recovered fibers, only 45 (0.006 percent) matched either target fiber. In these two studies, more comprehensive testing was done, including microspectrophotometry and TLC, in addition to comparison microscopy.

More recent studies have supplied similar, supporting information. A study of unrelated textiles from random criminal cases compared 2,043 fibers against one another. None of the fibers had the same optical properties and microscopic characteristics. These findings demonstrate that it is exceedingly rare for two fibers at random to have the same microscopic and chemical traits. Another study calculated the frequency of finding at least one red woolen fiber on a car seat at 5.1 percent; if more than five are found, however, the relative frequency plummets to 1.4 percent.

Fibers make good evidence for a number of reasons: They vary greatly, are easy to analyze, and are everywhere there are textiles. Fibers have figured prominently in many high-profile cases and are researched extensively by forensic and textile scientists alike. Textile fibers are one of the most frequently encountered types of physical evidence.

GLOSSARY

acetate a manufactured fiber in which the fiber-forming substance is cellulose acetate; where not less than 92 percent of the hydroxyl groups are acetylated, the term triacetate may be used as a generic description of the fiber

achromat a lens that is designed to limit the effects of chromatic and spherical aberration. Achromatic lenses are corrected to bring two wavelengths (typically red and blue) into focus in the same plane.

acrylic manufactured fiber in which the fiber-forming substance is any long-chain synthetic polymer composed of at least 85 percent by weight of acrylonitrile units

allele a variant form of a gene—the gene for eye color, for example, has various forms resulting in brown eyes, blue eyes, etc.

anagen the active growth phase of a follicle when it produces hair

analyzer a polarized filter that is placed in a microscope's light path

anidex a manufactured fiber in which the fiber-forming substance is any long-chain synthetic polymer composed of at least 50 percent by weight of one or more esters of a monohydric alcohol and acrylic acid

anisotropic the optical property of a material where its characteristics vary with direction or orientation; conceptually, the material has a "grain" to it and its properties vary

apochromat an apochromat, or apochromatic lens (apo), is a lens that has better color correction than the much more common achromat lenses

aramid a manufactured fiber in which the fiber-forming substance is any long-chain synthetic polyamide in which at least 85 percent of the amide linkages are attached directly to two aromatic rings

Becke line a rim of light visible along an edge in plane-polarized light because the specimen is acting like a crude lens, a Becke line can be used to determine if the refractive index of the specimen is higher or lower than the surrounding medium

birefringence the optical property of a material that has more than one refractive index and, therefore, the light rays passing through it differ in their velocity (the beams suffer unequal refraction during passage through the material, which is said to be doubly refracting or birefringent)

block polymers a chain of monomers made up of repeated homopolymers; spandex is an example of a block polymer

catagen the transitional growth phase of a hair follicle as it switches from actively growing (anagen) to resting (telogen)

chromophores the subunits of a molecule that preferentially absorb specific wavelengths of light, resulting in color

circumstantial evidence evidence based on inference and not on personal knowledge or observation

class a group of things that share one or more traits or characteristics; classes are hierarchical, such as the classes *golden retriever, all dogs, carnivores,* and *mammals*

color color is the visual perceptual property corresponding in humans to the categories called red, yellow, blue, black, etc.; color derives from the spectrum of light interacting in the eye

copolymers a polymer where two or more monomers compose the polymer chain

cortex the inner mass of a hair shaft made up of spindle-shaped cells, pigment granules, and other structures

cuticle outer layers of overlapping scales on a hair shaft

delustrant microscopic particles of material, typically titanium dioxide, introduced into a fiber as it is made to break up light that hits the fiber, reducing its brightness

denier a linear measurement based upon the weight in grams of 9,000 meters of a fiber

direct transfer the movement of material from A to B with no intermediaries (for example, a person stepping in mud directly transfers that material to the shoes)

DNA a polymer, deoxyribonucleic acid, that is found in nearly all living cells and contains the genetic information for an organism

dye a soluble colorant used to impart color to a material

eumelanin   the darker of the two pigments found in hair

evidence   information, whether in the form of personal testimony, the language of documents, or the production of material objects, that is given in a legal investigation, to makes a fact or proposition more or less likely

fabric   any planar material made up of fibers or yarns

fiber   a unit of matter that is at least 100 times longer than it is wide that can be used to create yarns or textiles

fluorescence   the luminescence of a substance excited by radiation

follicle   a hair follicle is the part of the skin that grows hair

frequency   the number of waves that pass a given point in one second; typically denoted by the symbol υ

genes   section of the DNA molecule that code for specific things; think of genes as words. The ordering of the genes provides the instructions to manufacture particular proteins (or sentences) in the body.

hairs   a fibrous structure in the skin of mammals

hertz   cycles per second

homopolymers   a polymer with one type of monomer that repeats itself

hot stage   a microscope stage filled with a heating elements so as to subject samples to increased temperature for chemical analysis

identification   placing a thing into a class, like *cocaine, baseballs,* or *black swans*

indirect transfer   the movement of material from A to B to C, with B acting as an intermediary (for example, a person walking with muddy shoes across a clean floor is the intermediary [B] between the mud [A] and the floor [C])

individualize   placing a thing into a class with one and only one member; uniqueness

infrared region   the range of the electromagnetic spectrum from 2,500 to 16,000 nm, with a corresponding frequency range from 1.9×10^{13} to 1.2×10^{14} Hz

isotropic   the optical property of a material where its characteristics are the same in all directions or orientations

knit fabric   a fabric constructed of interlocking series of loops of one or more yarns

known item   a thing or sample collected to intentionally represent itself; a cup of white powder taken from a previously sealed bag of flour is known to be that material

lens   a translucent material that bends light in a known and predictable manner

lyocell   a manufactured fiber composed of precipitated cellulose and produced by a solvent extrusion process where no chemical intermediates are formed

manufactured fibers   the various families of fibers produced from fiber-forming substances, which may be synthesized polymers, modified or transformed natural polymers, or glass

medulla   a variably-expressed series of hair cells that run along the central axis of a hair

melanocytes   the cells in a hair follicle that produce pigmentation (melanin granules)

metallic fiber   a manufactured fiber composed of metal, plastic-coated metal, metal-coated plastic, or a core completely covered by metal

metamers   a pair of colors that appear to be the same in one lighting condition but appear different in another

microscope   an instrument using multiple lenses that magnifies the image of a sample

microspectrophotometer   an instrument that measures the absorption or transmittance of specific wavelengths of light in the visible and ultraviolet ranges

mitochondria   subunits (organelles) of a cell that are responsible for, among other things, energy production

mitochondrial DNA   the genetic information contained within mitochondria; this DNA has a different structure than and is separate from the DNA in the nucleus of the cell

modacrylic   a manufactured fiber in which the fiber-forming substance is any long-chain synthetic polymer composed of less than 85 percent but at least 35 percent by weight of acrylonitrile units

monomer   the repeating chemical units of a polymer

natural fiber   fibers from animals, plants, or minerals that appear in the form in which they are found, with minimal to moderate processing

nonwoven fabric   an assembly of textile fibers held together by mechanical interlocking in a random web or mat, by fusing of the fibers, or by bonding with a cementing medium; felt is a common example

nuclear DNA   the DNA found in the nucleus of a cell

nylon   a manufactured fiber in which the fiber-forming substance is any long-chain synthetic polyamide in which less than 85 percent of the amide linkages are attached directly to two aromatic rings

nytril   a manufactured fiber in which the fiber-forming substance is any long-chain synthetic polymer composed of at least 85 percent of a long-chain polymer of vinylidene dinitrile where the vinylidene dinitrile content is no less than every other unit in the polymer chain

olefin   a manufactured fiber in which the fiber-forming substance is any long-chain synthetic polymer composed of at least 85 percent by weight of ethylene, propylene, or other olefin units

parfocality   the trait of a microscope where all lenses are in focus when each is placed in the light path. In turn, non-parfocal lenses require refocusing.

persistence   the retention of transferred evidence on a substrate

phaeomelanin   the lighter of the two pigments found in hair

pigments   insoluble colorants that must be placed inside or stuck to the outside of the thing they are to color

pleochroism   the variation of color of a specimen as it moves through different orientations of light

polarizer   a polarized filter that is placed in a microscope's light path above another polarized filter (the analyzer)

polyester   a manufactured fiber in which the fiber-forming substance is any long-chain synthetic polymer composed of at least 85 percent by weight of an ester of a substituted aromatic carboxylic acid, including but not restricted to substituted terephthalate units and para-substituted hydroxybenzoate units

proxy data   inductive evidence of a past event; indirect information

questioned item   an object or sample collected as potential evidence of association. A questioned item is an unintentional sample; for example, white powder taken from a crime scene must be tested to identify it (it could be flour, cocaine, or laundry detergent).

rayon a manufactured fiber composed of regenerated cellulose, as well as manufactured fibers composed of regenerated cellulose in which substituents have replaced not more than 15 percent of the hydrogens of the hydroxyl groups

refractive index the ratio of the speed of light in a vacuum to the speed of light in a medium; always greater than 1.0

saran a manufactured fiber in which the fiber-forming substance is any long-chain synthetic polymer composed of at least 80 percent by weight of vinylidene chloride units

spandex a manufactured fiber in which the fiber-forming substance is a long-chain synthetic polymer composed of at least 85 percent of a segmented polyurethane

spectroscopy the study of the interaction of light and matter

spherical aberration a deviation from the norm resulting in an image imperfection due to the increased refraction of light rays that occurs when rays strike a lens, or a reflection of light rays that occurs when rays strike a mirror near its edge in comparison with those that strike nearer the center

spinneret a showerhead-like device through which liquid polymer (spinning dope) is pumped to form fibers

spinning dope the liquid polymer used to make fibers; it is made through chemical formulation or the dissolving of materials

spot plate a ceramic tile with insets or divots to keep small samples separate and to allow chemicals to be added individually

telogen the resting growth phase of a hair follicle

tex a linear measurement based on weight per unit length equal to the weight in grams of 1,000 meters (1 km) of a fiber

transfer the movement of material from one location to another, either directly (A to B) or indirectly (A to B to C)

vinal a manufactured fiber in which the fiber-forming substance is any long-chain synthetic polymer composed of at least 50 percent by weight of vinyl alcohol units and in which the total of the vinyl alcohol units and any one or more of the various acetal units is at least 85 percent by weight of the fiber

vinyon a manufactured fiber in which the fiber-forming substance is any long-chain synthetic polymer composed of at least 85 percent by weight of vinyl chloride units

wave number   the inverse of the wavelength measured in centimeters; a wave number is 1 cm^{-1} (reciprocal centimeters)

woven fabric   fabrics composed of two sets of yarns and formed by the interlacing of these yarns

yarn   a continuous strand of textile fibers, filaments, or material in a form suitable for weaving, knitting, or otherwise entangling to form a textile fabric

FURTHER READING

Print

Bisbing, Richard E. "The Forensic Identification and Association of Human Hair." In *Forensic Science Handbook.* 2nd ed. Vol 1, edited by Richard Saterstein, 389–428. Upper Saddle River, N.J.: Pearson Education, 2002. An incisive article on the history and use of hair examinations.

Butler, John M. *Forensic DNA Typing: Biology and Technology Behind STR Markers.* Boston: Academic Press, 2001. This comprehensive handbook helps forensic scientists gain a better understanding of short tandem repeat (STRs) markers and the procedures needed to properly analyze them, while helping professionals in the law enforcement and legal communities comprehend the complexities of DNA profiling.

Caddy, Brian ed. *Forensic Examination of Glass and Paint.* Forensic Science Series. London: Taylor & Francis, 2001. An edited volume intended for practitioners, *Forensic Examination of Glass and Paint* covers the types of trace evidence in the title with a bit of a European view; the methods used in the United States may not be reflected entirely in all of the chapters. Although expensive, Caddy's book, like all of those in the Taylor & Francis International Forensic Series, is worthwhile for the serious student of forensic science.

Deadman, Harold. "The Importance of Trace Evidence." In *Trace Evidence Analysis: More Cases in Mute Witnesses,* edited by Max M. Houck. San Diego, Calif.: Elsevier Academic Press, 2004. Written by top practicing forensic scientists, this is one of an edited collection of cases that explain in detail the detective and analytic work that goes into solving complex cases.

Emsley, John. *Molecules at an Exhibition: Portraits of Intriguing Materials in Everyday Life.* Oxford: Oxford University Press, 1998. A well-known and well-published popularizer of chemistry, Emsley's writing could inspire almost anyone to become a chemist. This is one of his more popular books, and while broad in scope never misses an interesting detail or fact. Any of Emsley's books are a wonderful introduction to the "behind the scenes" of chemistry, but *Exhibition* is the best place to start.

Gerber, Samuel M., ed. *Chemistry and Crime.* Washington, D.C.: American Chemical Society, 1983. An illuminating view of forensic science in fact and fiction. Underlines the relationship between detective fiction and the development of modern forensics.

Gerber, Samuel M., and Richard Saferstein, eds. *More Chemistry and Crime.* Washington, D.C.: American Chemical Society, 1997. This book covers forensic disciplines and techniques such as detection of arsenic, forensic toxicology, dust analysis, examination of arson evidence, and DNA typing.

Houck, Max M., ed. *Mute Witnesses: Trace Evidence Analysis.* San Diego, Calif.: Elsevier Academic Press, 2001. Written by some of the top practicing forensic scientists, each chapter explains in detail the detective and analytic work that goes into solving complex cases.

———. *Trace Evidence Analysis: More Cases in Mute Witnesses.* San Diego, Calif.: Elsevier Academic Press, 2004. Continues and builds upon the tradition of its successful companion title *Mute Witnesses.* Written by some of the top practicing forensic scientists, each chapter explains in detail the detective and analytic work that goes into solving complex cases.

Houck, Max M., and Jay A. Siegel, Ph.D. *Fundamentals of Forensic Science.* New York: Elsevier Science, 2006. An acclaimed, comprehensive textbook of the forensic sciences for the professors and students of forensic science programs.

Murphy, Douglas B. *Fundamentals of Light Microscopy and Electronic Imaging.* New York: Wiley-Liss, 2001. Murphy provides the fundamentals of optics, light, and color while reviewing the central topics in light microscopy. The book is accessible and well-written. Murphy clearly explains the complex phenomena involved in microscopy without overdoing the formulae and math. The book addresses the most modern aspects of microscopy (digital imaging, for example) without ignoring the basics.

National Institute of Justice. *Forensic Sciences: Review of Status and Needs.* Gaithersburg, Md.: National Institute of Standards and Technology, 1999. Important report from the U.S. Department of Justice on the proposed issues and obstacles to education and training of forensic scientists. The report was updated in March 2006.

Robertson, James, and Michael C. Grieve, eds. *Forensic Examination of Fibres.* Boca Raton, Fla.: CRC Press, 1999. A very technical book aimed at the profession, this book nevertheless is a key resource for those who want to know more about fibers as evidence. The various chapters go into great detail about techniques and interpretation methods.

Robertson, James, ed. *Forensic Examination of Hair.* London: Taylor & Francis, 1999. Another book edited by the well-known forensic trace examiner, James Robertson, *Forensic Examination of Hair* is targeted at professional forensic scientists. The chapters cover growth, chemistry, microscopy, and interpretive methods for forensic hair examination.

Ryland, Scott, and Max M. Houck. "Only Circumstantial Evidence." In *Mute Witnesses: Trace Evidence Analysis,* edited by Max M. Houck. San Diego, Calif.: Academic Press, 2001. Written by some of the top practicing forensic scientists, each chapter explains in detail the detective and analytic work that goes into solving complex cases.

Schneck, William M. "Cereal Murder in Spokane." In *Trace Evidence Analysis: More Cases in Mute Witnesses,* edited by Max M. Houck. San Diego, Calif.: Academic Press, 2004. Written by some of the top practicing forensic scientists, each chapter explains in detail the detective and analytic work that goes into solving complex cases.

Thornton, John. "Ensembles of Class Characteristics in Physical Evidence Examination." *Journal of Forensic Sciences* 31, no. 2 (1986): 501–503. Thornton demonstrates, using .25 caliber firearms of a single manufacturer, how class characteristics in combination can more specifically identify evidence. This article neatly refutes the assumption that all class evidence should be interpreted as merely "could have" evidence.

Thornton, John, and Donna Kimmel-Lake. "Trace Evidence in Crime Reconstruction." In *Crime Reconstruction*, edited by W. Jerry Chisum and Brent E. Turvey. New York: Academic Press, 2006. An impressive working guide to the interpretation of physical evidence, designed for the forensic generalist and those with multiple forensic specialties.

Tridico, Silvana R. "Hair of the Dog." In *Trace Evidence Analysis: More Cases in Mute Witnesses*, edited by Max M. Houck. San Diego, Calif.: Academic Press, 2004. Written by some of the top practicing forensic scientists, each chapter explains in detail the detective and analytic work that goes into solving complex cases.

Waggoner, Kim. "The FBI Laboratory: 75 Years of Forensic Science Service." *Forensic Science Communications* 9, no. 4 (2007). An interesting essay on the history of this important bureau.

Wheeler, Barbara. "Who Do You Believe?" In *Trace Evidence Analysis: More Cases in Mute Witnesses*, edited by Max M. Houck. San Diego, Calif.: Academic Press, 2004. Written by some of the top practicing forensic scientists, each chapter explains in detail the detective and analytic work that goes into solving complex cases.

Web Sites

Organizations in Forensic Science

Note: Many of the following organizations meet each year, sometimes multiple times, around the United States. Many have student membership status and all of them provide additional information about their areas of interest on their Web sites.

American Academy of Forensic Sciences. URL: www.aafs.org. The American Academy of Forensic Sciences is a nonprofit professional society organized in 1948 that is devoted to the improvement, administration, and the achievement of justice through the application of science to the processes of law.

American Society of Crime Laboratory Directors. URL: www.ascld. org. The American Society of Crime Laboratory Directors (ASCLD) is a nonprofit professional society of crime laboratory directors and forensic science managers dedicated to promoting excellence in forensic science through leadership and innovation.

California Association of Criminalists. URL: http://www.cacnews.org. Recognizes and promotes achievements in criminalistics.

Microscopy Society of America. URL: www.microscopy.org. The Microscopy Society of America (MSA) is a nonprofit organization dedicated to the promotion and advancement of the knowledge of the science and practice of all microscopical imaging, analysis, and diffraction techniques useful for elucidating the ultrastructure and function of materials in diverse areas of biological, materials, medical, and physical sciences.

Mid-Atlantic Association of Forensic Scientists. URL: www.maafs.org. The mission of the Association is to encourage the exchange and dissemination of ideas and information within the fields of recognized forensic sciences through improving contacts between persons and laboratories engaged in the forensic sciences; stimulate research and the development of new or improved techniques; and promote high standards of performance and facilitate professional acknowledgment of persons working in recognized forensic science disciplines.

Midwest Association of Forensic Scientists. URL: http://www.mafs. net. The purpose of MAFS is to encourage the exchange of ideas and information within the forensic sciences by improving contacts between people and laboratories engaged in forensic science. Supports and stimulates research and development of new or improved techniques, and works to promote the improvement of professional expertise of persons working in the field of forensic science through education, scientific seminars, and research grants.

Northeastern Association of Forensic Scientists. URL: www.neafs. org. The Northeastern Association of Forensic Sciences (NEAFS) is a nonprofit regional organization of forensic scientists. Its stated purposes are to exchange ideas and information within the field of forensic science, and to foster friendship and cooperation among the various laboratory personnel, encourage a high level of competency among professionals in the field of forensic science, promote recognition of forensic science as an important component of the criminal justice system, and stimulate increased implementation of existing techniques, along with research and development of new techniques within the field, and to encourage financial support for these efforts.

Northwestern Association of Forensic Scientists. URL: www.nwafs. org. The Northwest Association of Forensic Scientists is a nonprofit organization that was formed to encourage the dissemination of information within the field of forensic science and discuss problems of common interest, foster friendship and cooperation among forensic scientists, and stimulate research and development of new techniques within the field.

Southern Association of Forensic Scientists. URL: www.southernforensic. org. The objectives of the Southern Association of Forensic Scientists are to encourage dissemination of information within the field of forensic sciences and to discuss problems of common interest; foster friendship and cooperation among forensic scientists; stimulate research and development of new techniques within the field; promote the use of standardized methodology and presentation of conclusions; to encourage compilation of statistical data of value in the field; assist in maintaining a high level of professional competence among practicing forensic scientists; and lend assistance to colleges and universities in the development of forensic science and related curricula and to law-enforcement planning agencies.

Southwestern Association of Forensic Scientists. URL: www.swafs.us. The Southwestern Association of Forensic Scientists (SWAFS) is a nonprofit organization that was formed to provide an association for persons who are actively engaged in the profession of scientific examination of physical evidence in an organized body so that the profession of all its disciplines may be effectively and scientifically practiced, exchange information among forensic scientists to improve techniques, encourage research in forensic science, and keep its members apprised of the latest techniques and discoveries in forensic science.

INDEX

Note: *Italic* page numbers indicate illustrations; page numbers followed by *t* indicate tables.

A

AATCC (American Association of Textile Chemists and Colorists) 99
absorbance 31
absorption maxima 31
acetate 86*t*
achromat 45–46
acrylic 86*t*, 92
addition reaction 91, 93
adenine (A) 76
Africans (ancestral group) 70
allele 77, 78
American Association of Textile Chemists and Colorists (AATCC) 99
anagen 64, 65, *65*, 72, 80
analysis, of evidence 21–23
analyzer (polarized light) 57
ancestry, hair and 70–71, 70*t*
anidex 86*t*
aniline dyes 100, 101
animal fibers 89–90
animal hair 67–68
anion 28
anisotropic material 55–58, *56*
apochromat 46–47
aramid 86*t*
archaeology 3
artificial silk 92
Asians (ancestral group) 70–71
association, comparison and 15
astigmatism 46
asymmetry, of science 17, 19
atoms, spectroscopy and 24, 30
Audemars, Georges 92
Avtex Fibers Incorporated 92

B

Bacon, Sir Francis 16–17
barrier filter 59–60
Barron, Arthur 38
base pairs 76, 77
Becke, Johann Karl 53
Becke line 53, *54*
bias in scientific observations 16–17
binocular microscope 44
birefringence 95
Bisbing, Dick 74
bleached hair 71
block polymers 89, *90*
body hair 68–70
bonded pairs 76
bulb root 64, 65

C

Carothers, Wallace 88
catagen phase 64, 65, *65*
cation 28
cellulosic fibers 85, 92
chameleon effect 100–101
characterization 32, 72
Charbonnet, Hilaire de 92
chemical analysis, of fibers 101–102
chemical bonds 33
chemical properties of fibers 103
chromatic aberration 46
chromophores 31–32
chromosomes 76, 77
circumstantial evidence 2
class characteristic 16
class/classification 8–10, 9*t*
  and individualization 104
  and known/questioned items 12
class evidence 104–105